Wealthy AND Wise

Also by Claude Rosenberg, Jr.

Stock Market Primer

The Common Sense Way to Stock Market Profits

Psycho-Cybernetics and the Stock Market

Investing with the Best: What to Look for, What to Look Out for in Your Search for a Superior Investment Manager

Wealthy AND Wise

How You and America Can
Get the Most Out of
Your Giving

Claude Rosenberg, Jr.

Little, Brown and Company
Boston   New York   Toronto   London

First Edition

Income from *Wealthy and Wise* will be directed to the Reach Out, Make A Difference Corp., which will in turn distribute it to nonprofit charitable organizations for their immediate use.

Library of Congress Cataloging-in-Publication Data
Rosenberg, Claude N.
    Wealthy and wise / by Claude Rosenberg.—1st ed.
      p.   cm.
    Includes index.
    ISBN 0-316-75741-1
    1. Philanthropists — United States.   2. Philanthropists — United States — Finance, Personal.   3. Community development — United States — Finance.   I. Title.
HV91.R675   1994
361.7'4'0973— dc20   94-7221

10   9

MV-NY

Published simultaneously in Canada by
Little, Brown & Company (Canada) Limited

Printed in the United States of America

To Weezy . . . Mutual love and respect, plus companionship and a sharing of common goals and values. Who could ask for anything more?

Contents

Acknowledgments — xi

Introduction — 3
*Good Fortune and Some Embarrassing
Confessions*

Chapter 1 — 11
Saving Our World Champion Country

Chapter 2 — 18
*Reaching Out — A Launching Platform
for America's Recovery*

Chapter 3 — 27
Found Money with Added Amenities

Chapter 4 — 34
*Money as a Route to Personal and
Family Fulfillment*

Chapter 5 — 45
Proving It Can Be Done

Chapter 6 — 49
*Breakthrough 1: How Spending Patterns
Affect the Ability to Save*

Chapter 7 — 55
*Breakthrough 2: Adding the Critical
Factor of Net Worth*

Chapter 8 — 67
Breakthrough 3: Identifying Your Financial Surplus

Chapter 9   71
Breakthrough 4: A Lifelong Financial
Statement

Chapter 10   83
Breakthrough 5: A Flexible Plan

Chapter 11   87
Point/Counterpoint: Separating Rational
and Less Rational Arguments For and
Against Greater Giving

Chapter 12   95
Protecting Yourself Against the Worst

Chapter 13   101
Breaking the Habit of Self-Deprivation

Chapter 14   106
Affording to Invest More in Yourself or
Your Community

Chapter 15   110
Maximizing the Time Value of Money

Chapter 16   117
Overcoming the Uncertainties of Net
Worth and Income

Chapter 17   121
How Lower-Income Groups Fit In

Chapter 18   129
Opportunities for Increased Giving by
Foundations and Businesses

Chapter 19   137
Propitious Timing for Using Your Capital

Chapter 20   141
Attractive Options for the Wealthy

Chapter 21   145
Getting Smarter About Your Giving

Chapter 22   151
Providing Adequately for Your Heirs

Chapter 23   161
The True Costs Associated with Charitable
Giving, Plus the Delicate Challenge of When,
if Ever, You Should Entertain Becoming a
Serious Giver

Chapter 24   166
Plausible Spending or Giving Levels for More
than 100 Different Income and Earning-Asset
Combinations, with Estimated Wealth Results

Chapter 25   175
How Much Healing of America Might Be
Accomplished? And How the Government
Might Provide Greater Incentives
to Private-Sector Contributors

Chapter 26   181
How Private Citizens Can Triumph over
Public Obstacles

Chapter 27   190
When Thomas Jefferson, Andrew Carnegie,
John Gardner, and Jimmy Carter Meet

Appendix   195

Index   197

Acknowledgments

FOUR years of thought, talk, and probing have involved countless individuals in the *Wealthy and Wise* effort. Original spreadsheet programs that constitute the basis for understanding surplus monies and financial affordability would not have been possible without David M. Jellison, along with Roxy Rorapauth Harte, Bryan McCann, Professor Gene Webb, and especially Dr. Jeffrey Moore and Tim Wei of Stanford University's Graduate School of Business, whose tireless spreadsheet and matrix work was a breakthrough unto itself.

Then there were friends and interested parties who requested and then critiqued numerous early versions of the manuscript. For this and other help, I am deeply indebted to social philosopher, leader, and author John Gardner, who wouldn't let me quit; investment consultant (and author) Charley Ellis; respected members of the philanthropic community Phyllis Cook, Steven Dobbs, Roger Heyns, Ira Hirschfield, Rob Johnston, Ed Nathan, Peter Seligmann, Bruce Sievers, Dwayne Silverstein, Nancy Wiltsek, and H. Peter Karoff; tax and related professionals Donald Seiler and Peter Maier; psychologist John Levy and author John O'Neil; author and consultant Louis Patler; Jay Hopkins, Nicholas Germanacos, and Fran Gendlin; numerous professionals, including Amy Gill and Barry Johnson, at the usually maligned IRS in

Washington, DC; Seth Reicher and Rob Parenteau; Elizabeth Robinson, who kept her smile through many edits; and Maris O'Neill, who witnessed the many conflicting moods that come with reedits; and personal friends Gerson Bakar, David Bourke, Albert Haas, and John Levin. And, of course, the one who allowed me the time and attention to pursue it all: wonderful Louise (Weezy). To all of the above and many more, my sincerest appreciation for your help and encouragement.

Wealthy AND Wise

Introduction

Good Fortune and Some Embarrassing Confessions

I'VE been lucky. I fortuitously chose a profession, investment management, in which opportunities were abundant. I worked hard, acquired some special skills, produced exceptional results for my clients and, in turn, for my business. And I invested wisely for myself and my family.

But some funny things happened on the road to prosperity, the strangest of which occurred as our income accelerated and our assets grew. In short, whatever targets we set for "sufficient" income or assets kept moving away from us. Hit one target and suddenly it seemed smaller than anticipated. Hit another and experience the same reaction. And ostentatious living was not the culprit; neither our tastes nor our needs were the least bit extravagant. Of course, inflation was a factor that kept raising our definition of financial adequacy, but this accounted for only part of our elusive goals.

Fortunately for us, the rising targets did not diminish our peace of mind. Unlike many others enjoying increasing wealth whom I had observed or heard about over thirty or forty years, we did not let our advancing goals interfere with what we thought was a healthy attitude about money and its constructive uses. We spent what we considered to be prudent, and we also discovered a positively contagious habit: the sharing of our good fortune with organizations devoted to deserving causes, especially those helping people less fortunate than us.

But I must confess that, despite my investment accomplishments, we were virtually flying blind with our finances. We hadn't modeled our spending to any percentage of our income. Nor had we disciplined ourselves adequately based on our asset accumulation. Finally, while we knew that our investments were growing rapidly, we hadn't concluded how much we might expect them to continue rising beyond our spending and our philanthropy. The fact was that we hadn't accurately calculated whether, under normal circumstances, we could expect to incur a deficit or a surplus from our earnings or our assets after deducting our outlays.

In other words, we lacked a specific, organized plan. The solid strategy I once thought we had developed for our finances wasn't solid enough. Too much guesswork was involved in all aspects, including our philanthropy, which I had assumed was extremely generous yet affordable.

This left me with two choices: I could either continue to close my eyes to reality or I could rethink our finances and become better educated about our options. I chose the latter, and one day I set out to prove for the first time what we could actually afford and how our money might be best allocated. I listed our income and the value of our assets, estimated the total investment returns that might be forthcoming over the next year or so from the earning portions of those assets, and then compared the results to a specific budget that included our needs, some luxuries, a reserve for our children's futures, and enough to cover our philanthropic outlays.

The conclusions were startling. It was as if I had literally found money. To my surprise, I discovered that we had dramatically understated our potential. We could afford to spend, or give, much more. Since we were basically happy with our standard of living, and since our income and our asset ownership left a sizable cushion for us, we concluded that we could have been sharing more of what we had. A lot more! So we weren't as generous as we had imagined.

It took some time for me to accept this conclusion fully. I wanted to go through life believing that our philanthropy was overly generous. But the facts were quite clear: we could have been doing more, we should have been doing more, and, in consort with others, we could indeed be making substantially greater improvements to our local community and to society in general.

So we took our own advice. We expanded our philanthropy regularly and soon learned that it was ever more pleasant to *reduce* our wealth moderately than it was to accumulate it.

Reducing wealth a pleasure? A pleasure when I was certain that others with financial means seemed to experience quite the opposite reaction? Indeed, a further personal confession is that — without statistical proof — I had suspected that the vast majority of wealthy people, including the very wealthiest, looked upon even slight *planned* reductions of their assets as a plague.

Having learned what I had about our personal finances, I now decided to determine whether I was correct about other people of means. Were they far less generous than they could afford to be? Could I safely state that others could have been doing more, too?

So I set out to document that I wasn't simply placing an unfair personal filter on something as delicate as other people's finances. If people, even wealthy ones, were worried about their money, how could I, without sufficient research, say they shouldn't be? One of my challenges, therefore, was to determine why financial peace of mind escapes so many people, and then to find an alternative for those who worry unnecessarily about their money. Perhaps, I thought, the new plan that had convinced me that we could do more would be helpful to others, too.

To say that I have seen inconsistencies in how people handle prosperity is an understatement. Although I have watched people spend money like the proverbial drunken sailor, I have more often seen people of means worry unnecessarily about their funds. I know multimillionaires who lose sleep over tiny outlays of capital and others who even deprive themselves and their families of basic necessities.

Probably none of this excessive prudence is surprising. There are millions of people who are well off — especially many widows and retired people — who deprive themselves in unnecessary and unpleasant ways. But harmful deprivations exist practically everywhere — at all ages and, again, in all wealth categories.

Certainly there are those who must truly scrimp, people with

low-to-medium income or net worth who must be ultraconserva-
tive in all types of spending. In addition, strange as it may seem,
there are also legitimate reasons to have empathy for those with
high earning power or asset ownership who worry about spending
or sharing their wealth.

Empathy for the rich? Well, not for all of them. But for many,
there are understandable arguments *for* caution and *against* increased spending. Protection for health needs, family emergencies, legacy goals, and even possible investment setbacks are but
four of many reasons for conserving resources. Furthermore, despite their riches, perhaps many wealthy people lack financial
sophistication or harbor insecurities about money: emotional traumas can, and often do, haunt even those with abundant finances.
So, the insecurities persist. Too many people with reasonable
wealth punish themselves — and others — unnecessarily. Too many
place themselves under undue stress. Too many miss out on contentment. And probably for one major reason: most people simply
haven't developed a strategy for their wealth.

The crux of the matter is people's perception of affordability —
their view of whether they possess a shortage or a surplus of money,
and by what margin. The definition of what should or should not be
spent depends, among other considerations, on four major criteria.
The first involves the *stability* and the *liquidity* of monetary sources
that might be tapped. Obviously, the more stable the source and
the easier it is converted to cash, the more prudent any spending
will be. Affordability also must be judged on the basis of *available
reliable income* and on *spending requirements*. And finally, affordability has to be judged on the basis of *net worth*, or (normally) the
value of earning assets owned after deducting related debts and excluding nonearning assets such as homes and possessions.

Net worth. Net worth — a critical figure that is generally more
significant than income, far less visible, much more often neglected, and consistently assumed (incorrectly, as it turns out) to
be almost untouchable.

Untouchable? Why, I questioned, should net worth be so untouchable? Especially since it normally dwarfs income and usually
constitutes the best guide when judging affordability. In fact, the

best assessment of both affordability and generosity comes not from determining how much one spends or gives in absolute dollars and not from a comparison to what others do, but rather from calculating how much net worth remains after money has been allocated. Past assessments of generosity have concentrated on percentage increases, trends, income availability alone, and other factors that simply miss the affordability criterion that includes net worth.

So I now set out to determine the discretionary spending potential of others, with net worth a critical variable. And I probed. I gathered government and research statistics on incomes, spending needs and savings, estate values, and related charitable contributions. I assessed IRS and other data from countless angles. I analyzed this and other external information and added my own insights on how to accumulate and then protect investments, capital, and income.

Yet each research path I took left me with inadequate insights into net worth. That was the missing variable. Judging what constitutes surplus capital was impossible without it. Although I had been able to prove affordability for my wife and me because I knew our asset values, the average net worth of all but the most visible of the highest income earners constituted a deep, dark secret. Not even the IRS knows a living person's total net worth.

So I probed even further. Working with reported income data, and using my own analytic training and the knowledge gained from many years of investment experience, I was finally able to estimate net worth of all tax-filing groups with reasonable accuracy. This was a critical discovery. One of many breakthroughs in financial thought and analysis, unveiling net worth values has allowed me to judge affordability potentials and to answer the question of the generosity — or lack of generosity — of others.

What I found was that, on average, most people have been giving far less than they could. My research resulted in a startling conclusion: the charitable donations of the IRS's top income group averaged less than *10 percent* of what they could safely afford! And a similar pattern existed for other income categories, particularly the higher earners.

All of this brought me back to my challenges: how to show people what is truly surplus money and how to provide them greater financial peace of mind. So, I developed a computer program that allowed an understanding of a person's financial situation over short and longer periods. I considered lifetime needs and bequests after death. I pored over additional IRS figures and extrapolated statistics on income, assets, living standards, and contributions. And I created a realistic model for people to use when considering their financial wherewithal — whether for better living for themselves or for enhanced giving to society.

The model is a conduit to a solid strategy for the use of money, for people of all tax brackets. For my wife and me, it proved to be a further revelation. Using the new format, we formed a more intelligent approach to our assets, to our family's needs, and to higher targets for what we might give away — all done with a greater sense of comfort than we had ever felt before. This led us to start our own charitable foundation, to focus on the needs of the young and the underprivileged, with special interest in education. And this we have done, to our great joy and sense of satisfaction. It has been one of the most rewarding emotional experiences of our lives.

Since then, I have gathered additional data and have developed more insights into the subject of financial adequacy, spending potentials, and affordability. And the conclusions I have reached are filled with fascinating opportunities for a large number of people — opportunities that extend far beyond charitable giving alone.

The focus of this book, then, is happiness — the happiness that comes from the comfort of understanding more about money, from possessing a better financial strategy, and from knowing what people of means can or cannot afford to spend on themselves or share with others.

Properly used, everybody wins. *Wealthy and Wise* provides significant strategies to help you make far better use of your resources and get much more out of life — while still benefiting society, and perhaps even eliminating the dismal conditions that exist in so many communities.

In fact, adopting the principles that follow will help you develop an acquired taste for giving — a habit certain to produce an array of constructive effects on our society. The results should

- bolster the US economy,
- make an impact on the countless inefficiencies that bureaucrats refuse to face and that politicians are reluctant to tackle,
- ultimately reduce governmental deficits,
- temper inflationary worries while increasing employment,
- lead to a healthier US dollar and stronger investment markets, and
- produce more satisfying lives for practically everyone.

So, if you are open to new and interesting financial facts and provocative ideas, if you are willing to consider using small amounts of an obvious asset that will deprive you of precious little, and if you are seeking a happier present while offering your heirs and others hope for a better future — just read on.

Chapter 1

Saving Our World Champion Country

AMERICA emerged from World War II by far the richest, most powerful nation in the world. The United States had an enormous advantage at the end of the war; practically all of Europe, the United Kingdom, Japan, and other powers were physically and financially ravaged, but the United States was not. Another advantage was the safety of our nation's political system and an economic philosophy that time has proved superior to other forms. It took many decades, but we overcame the challenge of communism and, in effect, won that war too.

While we retain significant military superiority and considerable influence abroad, we're now suffering serious and growing weaknesses at home. We have accumulated huge debts and more and more are seeing conditions crumble before our eyes. Our educational system is often ineffective: a 1993 Department of Education study concluded that over 80 million Americans — approximately 30 percent of our total population and 47 percent of the age groups surveyed — lack the ability to comprehend beyond the most elementary levels and lack the skills required in today's economy. In 1992 some 37 million inhabitants were living in poverty (definition: annual earnings of $14,335 for a family of four or $7,143 for an individual living alone). Homelessness is rampant in countless communities: people living in private doorways, in public parks, many of whom should be in hospitals or sanitariums and many of whom constitute a health hazard for countless others. Widespread crime and drug abuse seem uncontrollable. The FBI recently warned that 83 percent of all Americans can expect to become victims of crime in their lifetimes. Family lives are less cohesive and more frenetic. Despite improved methods of contraception, illegitimate births, particularly among teenagers, are a huge problem; in fact, an astounding 30 percent of American children are currently born out of wedlock. Excessive unemployment, an expensive health care system, and a plethora of other maladies are a confusing burden to our citizenry, a burden that is growing heavier every day.

This is not to say that subpar literacy and training, social unrest, poverty, and sickness aren't often realities within healthy, growing societies. The significance of the weaknesses depends on their proportion. But in the United States at this time, the proportions are growing at alarming rates. And while there is never a good time for such maladies, now is a particularly unpropitious moment, a moment when global competition demands that our standards compare more, not less, favorably with the strong, emerging countries that are threatening our competitive existence.

When our nation's internal problems are considered in conjunction with an oversize federal deficit and the widespread near-insolvency of many cities and states, the metaphor of a failing champion hits all too close to home. Indeed, were historian Edward Gibbon alive today, he might be writing a book called *The History of the Decline and Fall of the American Empire.*

Are there remedies for these troubles? Is there something that we citizens can do? And if so, where do we begin?

Varying solutions to these complex problems have already been proposed. The highly regarded author and professor Peter F. Drucker, for example, argues in favor of private-sector remedies and contends that "government has proved incompetent at solving social problems." The prominent economist Robert Heilbroner combines that same respect for private-sector capabilities with a plea for more public funds to overcome many of our weaknesses. Even President Bill Clinton, referring to his cabinet appointees in December 1992, said, "We can't look to government programs to solve all our problems. These appointees know the limits of what government can do, as well as what government must do." Time will tell whether his actions parallel these words.

Private citizens have become skeptical of governmental ineffectiveness. Many of us are frustrated with being pawns of bureaucrats and politicians and are dissatisfied with the government regulations and inefficiencies that impinge on us. We cannot expect utopia, but sitting on our hands or zipping up our pocketbooks is no answer, either: the private sector must somehow expand its involvement. It must combine its entrepreneurial know-how and enthusiasm with one all-important additional ingredient: capital.

Capital! Money! Now there's a challenge! With so many people and governmental entities financially strapped, can money possibly be the economy's elixir? Fortunately, with an improved ability to identify surplus money, it can. I intend to demonstrate that at least $100 billion a year can be raised in the private sector — an amount that, through increased and more effective charitable giving, could foster dramatic improvements in the crime, drug, educational, and other afflictions that are disrupting our present and impeding our future.

A tiny 1 or 2 percent of that $100 billion could have expanded the country's 1993 summer jobs program to an additional one and a quarter million youngsters. One hundred billion dollars is more than triple what the Department of Education spent in its 1991 fiscal year and also more than triple the amount spent by the Department of Housing and Urban Development. It is over fifteen times the government's 1992 estimated drug-enforcement-related expenditures. It is also about twice the amount the National Urban League has proposed for its "Marshall Plan for America" — an ambitious wish list that includes, among other items, reeducation and retraining of our work force along with the redress of our basic problems.

And pain is not a prerequisite to achieving this goal. Just the opposite. In fact, bringing this $100 billion to society's needs should produce broad, positive effects on our local, state, and federal finances and environments, while ensuring more productive lives for millions of people.

Is this too good to be true, a wild dream? Not at all. With proper preparation and planning, the dream can become a reality.

This book will introduce numerous major breakthroughs in financial thinking and modeling that demonstrate how more generous giving habits can be adopted without sacrifice or financial risk. I call them breakthroughs because they break through the old, traditional concentration on income and the narrow thinking about the use of wealth. In doing so, they should break through resistance to new ideas about charitable giving as well as more satisfying living. They even break through some of the fuzziness that has developed in our country's economic, political, and social thinking, and in the process they provide hope for vast improvement in our society.

The most important of these breakthroughs is the calculation of *net worth* for each IRS income grouping. Quantifying wealth is like describing the size of another person: if you communicate the height without the weight, or the reverse, you risk projecting a totally inaccurate picture. Assessing a person's wealth and the potential for sharing or spending should not be judged by income alone, but also by net worth, with consideration given to the stability and potential of each.

Unveiling the size of net worth opens new vistas to affordability potentials and improved judgment of how truly charitable each group is — or, particularly in the case of our nation's highest earners, is not. While Americans are far more generous with their money and charitable efforts than the citizens of other nations, we haven't come close to our potentials. Consider 1991 IRS data, typical of years 1987–1994, which show that the top income group averaged adjusted gross income (AGI), excluding capital gains, of approximately $1.8 million, and that these earnings were accompanied by my conservatively calculated $16 million estimate of their net worth (using earning assets only). Focusing here on charitable giving, the reported $87,000 average donation from these highest earners represented only 4.8 percent of their income with zero allocated to their net worth. Assigning none of the $87,000 to their income, these people gave a mere one-half of 1 percent of their net worth. And these figures are before tax savings.*

As you will learn, this top bracket group's donations do not reflect the conservative estimate that they own over seven times the asset wealth for each dollar of reported income than do lower bracket earners. You will see how this highest IRS income category, which donated an average of around $85,000 more than certain lower wealth groups, could well be exceeding the latter's giving by around $898,000. Instead of contributing approximately forty times what the lower-income earners give, they could afford to contribute almost 450 times as much. Oddly enough, the statistics show that many of the wealthiest taxpayers have actually retreated from charitable giving. For example, the top two IRS categories experienced a rise of over 80 percent in real family income from 1980 to 1991, compared to less than 5 percent for the median income family group. Yet the average charitable donation from the top group dropped 57 percent, from $201,000 to $87,000; and taxpayers earning $500,000 to $1 million decreased their contributions 61 percent, from $46,000 to $18,000. And these low donation numbers occurred in a year in which the S&P Stock Index produced total investment returns exceeding 30 percent. Ironically, generosity from the most wealthy has diminished even though they probably stand to gain substantially from increased sharing.

My guess is that these affluent groups *aren't* simply selfish. Personal distractions, procrastination, the difficulty of sorting out how to deal with the many complex social issues at hand, and lack of confidence that their money can make an impact combine to

---

*Mathematical averages can, of course, be misleading. If one of ten people donates $900,000, and five give $20,000 each, for a total of $100,000, while four contribute nothing, the $100,000 average of the ten hardly represents typical experience. Numerous studies on charitable involvement conclude that giving from the high end is, as in this example, very uneven: small numbers of very generous contributors are usually offset by numerous low givers. Despite such disparities, the use of averages is valuable for the illustrative and educational purposes of this book.

interfere with the best of intentions. Better habits and processes need to be established, which in our case can come from clearer definitions of surplus funds and, equally important, from greater understanding of how strategic approaches to philanthropy can produce dramatic results.

Money alone will not solve our problems. All sorts of bureaucratic and political obstacles exist, and the private sector needs to improve its effectiveness, too. This book provides the ingredients to overcome many of these obstacles. You will learn about plans and strategies that can produce a new and constructive movement in this country that is bound to benefit you, your family, and your community. Great progress and excitement are in store. Changes must occur, and larger funds that are accompanied by greater efficiencies can substitute strength for weakness, order for chaos, beauty for ugliness. Indeed, providing lifetime opportunity for our communities and ourselves is the opportunity of a lifetime.

I will document the risk associated with increased expenditures. In most cases, it is so small as to be virtually insignificant. Despite the desperate realities of undergiving, nothing will be recommended that isn't prudent and conservative. Any and all recommendations will be shown to be manageable, so that concerns over wealth depletion can be mitigated.

I will also present ideas for additional tax deductions and other incentives our governments should consider to encourage sharing that will allow the private sector to remedy more effectively what the politicians have largely bungled. It is shortsighted for politicians and government not to cooperate more.

It is also shortsighted for private citizens to ignore the strong defensive considerations of all this. For instance, enlightened giving may be the best protection against confiscatory taxation, an inevitable response by our local, state, and federal governments to the problems we face. If the recent trends of growing maladies and massive deficits continue, the temptation will persist to consider new or higher taxes, or both. So it makes great sense for people with higher wealth to step up voluntarily now, while they can select the causes themselves and control more of the methods for addressing the issues. If they wait too long, they will no doubt be taxed to accomplish these ends in less productive ways.

Finally, my breakthroughs can be applied toward living better. As mentioned earlier, there are countless Americans, including the wealthy, who suffer needlessly, who can spend more yet live more happily and productively than they do now. Without encouraging ostentatious living, my model shows how people can live far more comfortably than they may have thought possible. Thus, a flexible plan is presented for both enhanced giving and enhanced living. After considering both, the model provides a method for determining approximate wealth into the future, including allowance for inheritance planning.

The fact is that many people who regularly think, "I can't afford it," really can — and with a minimum of sacrifice or risk. Many people regularly imagine affordability problems that simply don't exist. In some cases, the misperception causes few problems, but in other instances, it may deprive them, their families, and their communities of significant advantages. Thinking in family terms, for example, doesn't it make more sense to leave slightly less money (and it need be only a little less) to heirs who might live in a relatively trouble-free, greatly improved, safer country than to leave only slightly more to them and have them face a deteriorating, perhaps even dangerous, society? For so many, it is no longer appropriate to say, "I can't afford it." Rather, those of means should say, "I can't afford not to!"

Converting this "can't afford" attitude and its lost opportunities into more productive options is the central aim of this book. Many of America's worst domestic problems can still be solved — and we can't afford *not* to. But we must get to it now, before we become even weaker. A new proactive philanthropy can eliminate inefficiencies that are costing us dearly and obstructing progress. Indeed, new, more effective philanthropy is a powerful way to help our country retain its championship crown.

Chapter 2

Reaching Out — A Launching Platform for America's Recovery

ECONOMIC matters obviously influence social and political philosophies. Our country's democratic principles, for example, are partly based on the concepts of free enterprise. More recently, commencing with the decade of the 1970s but more actively pursued from 1981 through 1992, legislation and tax policies in the United States were heavily influenced by a "New Economics," also called "Reaganomics," "Supply-Side," or "Trickle Down" economics. The heart of this philosophy centered on less governmental involvement and on sharply lower tax rates that were expected to stimulate the economy enough to benefit all income groups. With this prosperity, Trickle Down anticipated sufficient tax revenues to lower, and perhaps even balance, our governments' budgets (local, state, and federal).

Driven in part by these principles, the United States enjoyed a long cycle of economic growth from 1982 to 1989. Yet even this robust period was accompanied by massive increases in budget deficits, along with serious infrastructure and social problems that left many people with a lower quality of life and with apparently dismal prospects. Then, starting in 1989, the economy suffered several years of a painful recession that further aggravated both the deficits and the pain.

Many contend that the Trickle Down policies lacked sufficient time to prove themselves, and others blame the outcome on selective tax hikes that occurred during President George Bush's term. Perhaps the most compelling excuse for Trickle Down's shortfalls was the concerted effort by US businesses throughout the 1980s and early 1990s to reduce their costs and improve their competitive positions. Significant layoffs of both white-collar and blue-collar workers led to widespread unemployment; and this, plus the tax cuts and the most pervasive series of corporate accounting write-offs in US history, reduced tax revenues and led to steadily climbing governmental budget deficits.

The fact is, however, that Trickle Down's record did not match its stated objectives. While there were many beneficiaries of this era, especially in higher wealth categories, not enough trickled down to others. We shouldn't ignore Trickle Down ideas, however.

Trickle Down unfortunately neglected a key principle that could have improved its results — the principle that an assured and potentially powerful trickling down would occur if the most advantaged recipients of lower taxation shared more of their good fortune with others. Since lower tax rates entailed smaller deductions for charitable contributions, there was an even greater need to encourage donations, and yet the urgings seldom surfaced. Frankly, had the tenets of this book been adopted more widely, the trickling down would surely have increased and the country would surely be better off.

Is it too late for such improvements to occur, given the political change of 1992 and President Clinton's initial program of increasing taxation in the highest brackets while lowering the AGI levels at which taxpayers started incurring the higher levies?* Won't reducing after-tax incomes only diminish incentives, reduce business formation and expansion, lower employment, and hamper overall prosperity?

High tax rates have generally been unfavorable for both the economy and the stock market. Assuming that this behavior repeats itself, about the best one can hope for is that the hikes will be short-lived or that the competitive juices of human beings, their survival instincts, their desires for accomplishment, to say nothing

---

*Federal rates should not be the sole criterion. Local and state levies, plus all sorts of taxes that impact spending or reduce incentives, are obviously critical.

of the human elements of ego and even greed, will prevail. And that people will continue to work hard to earn money, accumulate capital, invest in businesses, and attempt to elevate their economic positions. We have to hope that the renowned economist John Maynard Keynes's conclusion that businesspeople ultimately set their capital-spending levels based on "animal spirits" rather than on interest rates will overcome the burdens of higher taxation. Perhaps enough trickling down can occur from the human tendencies to succeed, provided that it is accompanied by a broader and more efficient adoption of sharing.

Enter "Reaching Out"

It is not too late for improvement. It can be as productive for the high end to share more now as it would have been throughout the 1981–1993 span. In fact, it can be even more productive — which is where "Reaching Out" comes in. Reaching Out calls on America's most fortunate to spearhead a revitalization of our country through enhanced and more involved philanthropy. Reaching Out is not only about giving more, which evidence shows the wealthy can well afford, but also about giving more strategically and effectively while encouraging more active volunteerism, too. Reaching Out is a plan for citizens to lift selective social burdens off the government's weary shoulders. It recognizes that ultimately the success of the United States depends on those higher up the economic ladder *reaching out* to those below, and that the greatness of America must be in *all* its people.

Thus Reaching Out is both reactive and proactive. It is the epitome of free enterprise as it enlarges private-sector involvement and its efficiencies; it is bound to reduce many maladies that exist in our country; it increases opportunity for our disadvantaged; it even enhances the prospects for ultimate deficit reductions and at least a stabilizing of tax rates for the very groups whose donations are most responsible for the achievements, assuming that the results ultimately supplant government expenditures. It is also the hope for balancing local budgets and for reducing their dependence on the federal government.

Deficit reduction is a claim that demands clarification. Certainly economic prosperity and its related tax receipts constitutes the least onerous route to balanced budgets, but it hasn't worked for decades. Lower spending at federal, state, and local levels is another popular avenue, but even the relatively light attention to this has weakened enough programs for the underprivileged and infirm to produce an expanded group of destitute people whose plights are further interfering with the living conditions of others.

Cost cutting and greater efficiencies in the public sector simply must occur, and the capital and competency of Reaching Out should become the catalysts for a reinvention of how government provides services. Sad as it is to believe, a constituency exists that benefits from a continuation of our problems. As Robert L. Woodson, founder and president of the National Center for Neighborhood Enterprise, a nonprofit that has been dealing successfully with education, crime prevention, and economic development of low-income communities, stated to me: "Too many livelihoods depend on bloated, inefficient programs, the kind that exist in socialist environments, the kind that are enigmatic to free market economies." Reaching Out should also prove that the private sector can accomplish more with less and lead to a more determined balanced-budget philosophy.

Adding More Effective Leadership to Philanthropy

We know that money alone will not solve our problems. The private sector needs to improve its effectiveness if it is to overcome the many obstacles that exist. Thus, stronger leadership is integral to my plan for Reaching Out. In short, those who give must demand that their capital receives stronger management — management that knows how to apply the pressures so often required to achieve positive results, management that recognizes that throwing money at problems with systemic weaknesses may only prolong their existence.

Too many communities are in trouble. And too many governmental organizations and special-interest groups are serious obstacles to the much needed remedies. Too many services provide inadequate value in exchange for the costs involved. Too many are directly or indirectly costing their users, including the taxpayers, too much. Perhaps the roadblocks are onerous governmental regulations or entrenched, selfish interest groups; perhaps they are stifling work rules or simply an obstructive legal system that can cause interminable delays and hold progress at ransom. Whatever the causes, now is the time for the public sector, including civil servants and other groups, to improve their effectiveness. Certainly many nonprofits — both operating charities and private foundations — require their own internal surgeries and stronger management, too. Like American businesses, most of which have already shaped up or are in the process of doing so, governmental and nonprofit managements and their personnel have to recognize their shortcomings and become more competitive, too.

Improvements will not occur easily, however. (Consider how many of the 1984 Grace Commission's recommendations to cut 14 percent of federal spending have been studiously avoided.) Politicians will be only so helpful, if they will cooperate at all, which leaves the private sector to become the catalyst for these essential changes. But being a catalyst will not be enough, either. Philanthropic leadership must become more aggressive with those who are blocking progress and those who can effect change. Nonprofits, too, must become more demanding of themselves. They need to develop improved judgments of their own capabilities. They need to supplant the soft criteria normally used to judge their successes: for example, they need to quantify their efficiencies much as for-profit businesses analyze returns per employee, returns on investment and on equity, profit margins, and the like. Donors have to be more creative to prepare people to help themselves, to reward personal efforts, initiative, and personal and family responsibilities. The leaders need to toughen their stance where necessary and be willing to tie forceful, constructive stipulations to their grantmaking. Heavy negotiations and strong bargaining by the larger donors may be needed to persuade those opposed to new approaches and increased efficiencies.

San Francisco's Delancey Street Foundation serves as a great inspiration for anyone motivated to overcome community or human problems, and for anyone seeking the related attainment of personal satisfaction that should accompany such involvement.

The organization's accomplishments also illustrate how outdated attitudes and entrenched systems may need to be bypassed and even eliminated in order to succeed.

Delancey provides a dramatic success story in the rehabilitation of felons, drug addicts, prostitutes, and other social outcasts. From its formation, the group took the controversial stand that the accepted remedies of interdiction and incarceration were ineffective. It had to buck many people whose personal interests hinged on prolonging drug availability or in keeping prisons full. It had to fight local residents, who feared that Delancey's "school for scoundrels" (to quote its leader, Mimi Silbert) endangered their safety. And without relying on traditional sources of funds, it found other ways to pay for its services. It prospered in a typical American way — through personal initiative and hard work. In Reaching Out terms, it chose the private-sector route to overcoming systemic obstacles. It chose imaginative, positive ways to succeed.

Delancey does not rely on philanthropic support. Self-sustaining financially, with no government funds, its four geographically dispersed centers have helped more than ten thousand people switch from human disasters into worthwhile citizens. The San Francisco facility alone is a model of accomplishment. It combines dignified living quarters, a training center, and a commercial establishment (a restaurant). It is an attractive compound, an asset to its city; it is also the headquarters for several other successful businesses, all started from scratch, that support its activities. Building this, however, required heavy negotiations with civic organizations, labor unions, and businesses alike — all of whom ultimately cooperated and today look at the results with joint pride. Delancey's success has finally attracted the federal government's attention: Lee Brown, director of the Office of National Drug Control Policy, is now attempting to ascertain how Delancey's methods of rebuilding lives through teaching people to be responsible and accountable can be built into a nationwide strategy. The words of Mimi Silbert also prove how curing ills can be a conduit to unique personal fulfillment. Asked about the secret to Delancey's achievements, Silbert emphasizes that residents "want what every human being desires: they want to be somebody." And asked why she personally does her job, she stresses the enhancement of her life through the joy of

helping others. In a lesson to anyone who is looking for a more ful-
filling life, she notes that her devotion allows her to feel like a
"somebody," too. Down deep, don't most of us seek an identity as a
worthy human being, with a want to be needed and a hope that we
can help and please others, too?

Another example shows how many businesses have contributed
their management experience and strong leadership, along with
money, to push structural changes in education. The Melville Innovations Grants Program combines direct grants to schools with
specialized training and technical assistance. Through a competitive process, Melville awarded three-year grants of up to $50,000
annually to nine schools throughout the Northeast that demon-
strated a commitment to fundamentally rethinking the way in
which they educate students. Melville employees are also lending
their expertise to the schools, including training teachers in human
relations skills, facilitating team meetings, and creating new curriculum materials. The schools — which represent a diversity of
communities, including urban, suburban, and rural; rich and
poor; white, African-American, Asian, and Hispanic — meet in
twice-yearly conferences where they share their successes and introduce one another to alternative methods of education.

There are many Delancey Street and Melville-type operations
across America. Look for them in your community.

To repeat, however, it isn't only government-controlled systems
that need to change. While most of the nation's foremost charitable organizations require little or no alteration, some are in need
of a refocus, too. Some have lost their spark, some have become
inefficient, some are producing poor returns to their contributors.
Many will only entertain constructive change when their major
donors demand better results from them.

In fact, we have to be careful not to glamorize nonprofit organizations instinctively. There are large differences in goals and
purposes that exist under the government's definition of nonprofits. Many nonprofits have become big businesses whose goals are
essentially commercial and whose tax exemption is very costly to
taxpayers. In 1993, the *Philadelphia Inquirer* ran a six-part series
entitled "Warehouses of Wealth: The Tax-Free Economy" that explained how many nonprofits are hardly charities at all. Staff writ-

ers Gilbert Gaul and Neill Borowski observed that "America's non-profit economy has become a huge, virtually unregulated industry" with considerable abuses, including high salaries, low efficiencies, and questionable goals. Needless to say, references to nonprofits in this book relate to those making true philanthropic grants and efforts for worthwhile and needy causes.

It should be clear that I'm not advocating excessive power to the monied. But our society must find ways to overcome narrow interest groups that are hampering progress, and enlightened, forceful philanthropy may be the most logical route to winning essential battles that are being lost today. Such leadership can also raise community consciousness about the reasons that problems exist and, in the process, create a larger constituency for change. Overall progress will also entice greater numbers of enthusiastic volunteers and attract widespread donations from smaller contributors.

Add to this momentum a greater concentration on local causes and you have the makings of a powerful economic, social, and political movement. Consider the potential of even small portions of the $100 billion figure mentioned earlier being allocated annually to regional needs, where meaningful improvements can become visible more quickly — certainly faster than can be achieved nationally — if proper leadership accompanies the capital.

There are countless communities where very small numbers of people — perhaps a half dozen or a dozen — could virtually turn their local environments around. And these prospects are not limited to small towns: with the special support of as few as two or three dozen families, communities of several million people could readily initiate programs that within a few years could better educate and train their youngsters, clean up their streets, greatly improve other needy conditions, and provide greater opportunities for their inhabitants. Later I'll present specific guidelines for local Reaching Out organizations such as these.

Reaching Out as a Philosophy for Our Time

So Reaching Out with capital and enlightened leadership is a fresh, practical approach to healing America's wounds and strengthening our nation. With proper organization and a willingness to do battle where required, contributors can succeed as never before and in the process achieve significant personal rewards. While sharing insignificant portions of their wealth, the major donors can benefit from the joys of making a difference and the knowledge that they are creating a more positive environment for their families, friends, and communities.

Reaching Out's success in elevating the quality of life and strengthening local communities can then produce enough positive momentum to our national economy to ensure not only that the United States can *survive* but that it can *revive*.

Reaching Out's combination of capital and leadership should, therefore, fit into the platforms of both major political parties, perhaps encouraging additional incentives from our government. As mentioned, I will present ideas for such constructive changes in tax legislation and government policies, as well as advice on how to be smarter and more effective in your giving. But the greatest impetus should come from the spirit and the Golden Rule principles that originally guided our forefathers in the writing of our Constitution and the Declaration of Independence — a philosophy that made the United States such a paragon of success.

And, Finally, the Importance of the Proof of Affordability

Expanding philanthropy obviously demands more than emotional, patriotic, or even improved-management pleas. The money has to be there, as it can be when its owners feel confident that it will be productive and especially when they feel comfortable that its absence will not be harmful to themselves. Thus, the path to greater generosity should be smoothed considerably as people learn how very affordable such sharing can be. The lessons to follow will reassure people of reasonable means that they can subdue their financial insecurities. They can follow constructive plans that allow them to continue investing their dollars while simultaneously pursuing the affordable and potent investment that well-managed philanthropy can be.

Chapter 3

Found Money with Added Amenities

ARGUING that somebody else's money should be given away is easy. It is also potentially presumptuous and can lack proper empathy. Fortunately, however, there are safe, comfortable ways to employ capital so effectively that it can provide greater satisfaction than many of the traditional asset-enhancement strategies people have sought over the years.

A starting point is to recognize that giving and contributing do not have to carry the negative connotations of money gone forever. Oh, some portions will prove unproductive. As with any investing, some philanthropy will seem fruitless. But this is no reason to ignore it. Living without conscience in a society riddled with problems is to almost everyone's eventual detriment. For one thing, it isn't smart to allow widening gaps between the "haves" and the "have-nots" in a society. Won't this inevitably lead to greater risks for everyone: the risks of widespread disillusionment, heightened crime, higher government spending, and lost potential for our families? Won't these maladies ultimately affect those in the most favorable circumstances today? As former Harvard president Derek Bok said, "If you think education is expensive, try ignorance."

We know what the billions of underutilized, surplus dollars can do for our society. But what can the sharing of such resources mean for the contributors? For openers, the constructive financial habits of Reaching Out will

- produce better decisions about what to do with money and when to do it;
- encourage intelligent, tax-effective use of money during their lifetimes and for eventual estate planning; and
- serve as strong, happy examples for family, friends, and others.

There are additional positives to consider, the first of which relates to the timing associated with the source of any delicate dipping into discretionary income or capital. The unequivocal fact is that bond and stock markets taken together have produced dramatically higher total (and "real," adjusted for inflation) returns in recent years than they have historically. While real estate markets have faltered badly since the mid-1980s, Chart A shows that ten-year annualized real returns from bonds and stocks since the early 1980s have averaged well above the results since 1936. Such prosperity suggests that greater generosity is distinctly affordable and that it may even be timely.

Recent returns are not the sole reason for the probable timeliness. Both fixed-income and equity markets are also facing the obstacle of high-priced starting points. This includes higher prices for bonds in relation to interest income, and higher prices for stocks in relation to earnings, cash flows, dividends, and book values. The combination of these elevated valuations plus the superior recent returns should at least mitigate the fear that money being used for philanthropy is coming from a depressed source.

Another reason why timing may be propitious involves tax savings. The elevated 1993 and 1994 tax rates result in higher write-offs from charitable donations, thereby encouraging philanthropy.

Of course, there are counterarguments to consider. One is that gifted money may reduce personal savings and possibly stifle the economy. If my recommendation were for heightened contributions from all wealth sectors, this would be a legitimate worry. But this is not my position. Emphasis here is on truly surplus wealth that, absent enhanced philanthropic gifting, will mainly build further wealth. But won't any dollars steered away from business in-

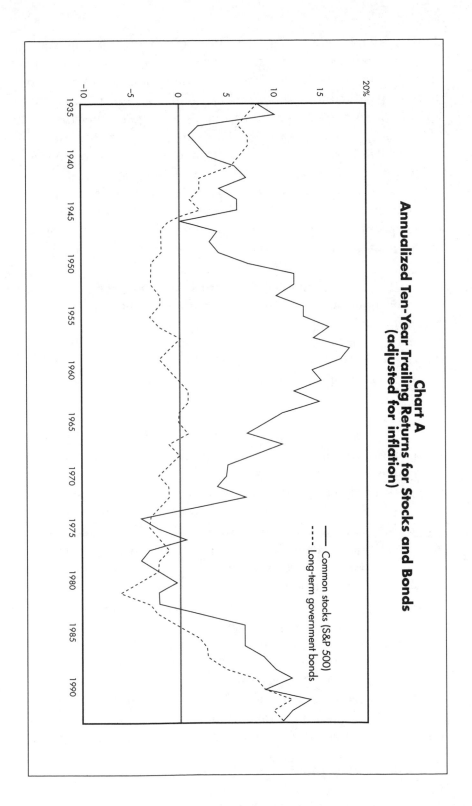

Chart A
Annualized Ten-Year Trailing Returns for Stocks and Bonds
(adjusted for inflation)

Common stocks (S&P 500)
Long-term government bonds

vestments reduce the economy's potential? Not if a Reaching Out sharing constitutes a productive investment itself. Also, not if the donation amounts leave ample room for both profit-making and nonprofit enterprises. The fact is that wise giving can actually bolster the economy. This is because, at today's tax rates, two and a half to three dollars of impetus to the economy can, *if properly directed,* occur from every dollar of tax deduction taken. A one-dollar contribution might cost the Treasury about thirty to forty cents in lost revenues, but every philanthropic dollar that flows directly into the economy obviously adds considerably more in the way of services. (The trouble is that many charitable contributions are "warehoused" and do not aid the economy immediately — something to be discussed later.)

Finally, there is the important question of whether it is valid to expect an elimination of our most glaring weaknesses should the private sector supplant public programs. A response comes from Peter F. Drucker in his December 19, 1991, *Wall Street Journal* article entitled "It Profits Us to Strengthen Nonprofits."

> Virtually every success we have scored has been achieved by nonprofits. . . . The nonprofits have the potential to become America's social sector. . . . There are now some 900,000 nonprofits, the great majority close to the problems of their communities . . . [and] there are now some 90 million Americans working as "volunteers."

Drucker says that nonprofits have produced the greatest advances in health and longevity, in rehabilitation of addicts, in prisoner reform, and in whatever improvements are occurring in inner-city schooling. He argues strongly for tripling the productivity of this nonprofit sector. And, as might be expected, he suggests that our citizens need to increase their donations to these organizations.

Drucker may be overly harsh on governments, which handle many programs well and are the last resort for other needs, and he may even exaggerate some of the advantages of nonprofit versus public forces — but it is hard to argue with his general conclusions. In addition to the efficiency arguments, donors can act quickly and creatively to stimulate nonprofits to achieve better results from the money donated, and they can concentrate their giving to causes and regions of their choice; and, of course, they can enjoy a greater sense of involvement and satisfaction than they derive from simply writing checks to the IRS or to equally impersonal state or local governments.

Numerous additional advantages should also occur from the improvements in sentiment and confidence that can result from wise and substantially elevated giving. Consider the broad impact of the following possibilities and the psychological lift that would occur throughout the country:

- Consumer spending would increase, as would business investment in capital spending and, of course, in people.
- The need for less government spending would reduce inflation worries and, in turn, might reduce interest rates. These lower money costs suggest a more competitive business picture, again, with higher employment.
- Higher business profits and elevated personal income would produce large tax revenues — the least painful way to reduce deficits.

Not only could our economy be strengthened through a widespread Reaching Out, but this in turn could encourage higher valuations for many US investment vehicles. Price-earning multiples on stocks could rise, making equity financing cheaper and leading to higher net worth for many shareholders, especially for many of the very individuals who helped initiate this renaissance. Even real estate, currently a laggard asset, would surely benefit from renewed confidence in the economy.

How many people would it take to produce the potential $100 billion annual impetus to private-sector investing? My calculations indicate that about 90 percent of it would come from approximately 3.4 million of the nation's 115 (1991) million taxpayers. In fact, a mere 51,000 of these taxpayers could account for an annual $40 billion alone.

The data are clear, the numbers undeniable: potential giving of this magnitude exists, is practical, and can have dynamic positive effects on our entire society. As an example, let's consider education, the backbone of the country's future, and see what enhanced private giving could accomplish.

To begin with, there were roughly 60,000 K-through-8 public schools in the United States in 1992, and 20,000 for students in grades 9 through 12. A $100 billion amount would provide an average of $1.25 million to each of these 80,000 learning institutions. There were 29.7 and 11.3 million students, respectively, in these schools — so $100 billion would provide approximately $2,500 per student per year, roughly a 50 percent supplement to the average of $5,000 per student being expended today.* Combining even small fractions of these dollars with Reaching Out effectiveness could have a sizable impact on our country's outlook. Assigning only one quarter of 1 percent of the $100 billion to a program like the Teen Outreach Program (TOP) is another example of money put to good use. A project of the Association of Junior Leagues International, TOP combines student-selected volunteer work with supportive classroom discussions to enhance problem-solving capabilities, teach solid approaches to daily living, and build confidence in the students. Advantages to communities receiving this volunteerism are important, but the major benefits are the well-documented impacts that TOP has made: the nonprofit's 1984–1991 record shows a 33-percent-lower pregnancy rate and a 50-percent-lower school dropout rate for TOP participants compared to non-TOP students. For annual costs averaging around $100 per participant, a $250 million allotment could serve two and a half million of the eleven million US public high school students.

Or consider another example, the federal government's Project Head Start program, which has, since its inception in 1965, provided comprehensive educational, health, and developmental services for children from low-income families. Just 10 percent of our $100 billion could raise enrollment from fewer than 700,000

---

*Gene Lang's widely publicized "I Have a Dream" program to prepare underprivileged children for higher education calls for a $1,000-per-student annual expenditure (obviously applicable to only a fraction of our students). This is not to promote this one approach over many others, but it does provide another basis of comparison.

children to almost 2.4 million (assuming the necessary cooperation is forthcoming from the related families).

So resources do exist to overcome the seemingly hopeless
problems that afflict so many American lives, and a widespread development of Reaching Out habits can improve the prospects for
one and all.

Chapter 4

Money as a Route to Personal
and Family Fulfillment

SOME readers may be thinking that none of this "giving by the wealthy" pertains to them. It is true that the thrust of my giving suggestions relates more to the relatively few in the very highest financial brackets than to the hundred-plus million of other taxpaying households in this country. But all groups can benefit from the Reaching Out philosophy, and almost everyone has some responsibility to do something, however small. While the "biggest bucks" will come from the very wealthy, others making relatively small contributions can, collectively, make a big difference, too. Reaching Out should also set the right standards for a considerably larger, younger group that is soon destined to dictate our country's future and is slated to receive by far the largest inheritance in our nation's history (an estimated $6 trillion to $10 trillion). In addition, philanthropy is one exception to the adage about the love of money being the root of all evil: philanthropy can be a root of happiness, as it provides a route to personal fulfillment.

Special Bonuses for the Benevolent

How can the gratification that this book describes be realized? The first step is a better understanding of surplus money. This knowledge will produce a sort of relaxation and engender greater financial peace of mind. And the fact that greater generosity might eventually reduce governmental deficits and even possibly current and future taxation should also help.

But these thoughts may not be sufficient. They may seem too passive, overly idealistic, or even too defensive to add momentous joy to our lives. Actually, there is no reason to think passively, idealistically, or defensively about philanthropy. So let's shift to something proactive, practical, and pleasing. Let us assume that those who can afford it deserve to treat themselves to "selfish" personal pleasures, satisfaction, and out-and-out gratification.

Am I suggesting that enlightened philanthropy can produce greater happiness than, for example, personal spending? The answer is a definite yes, with the proviso that the sharing does present some challenges.

One task is to subdue two annoyances that face most people with money (and many without much wealth as well). Let's face it: many of us are overwhelmed by countless mailings and by pleas for financial support from all quarters. Thus, a person who donates might fear being open to even more solicitations and the annoyance of having to say no to more and more pleas. After all, no one person can (or should) give to every cause. But there are ways to convert nuisance to satisfaction.

The starting point is to change the angry reaction that is common among people who receive regular requests for giving. In a way, responding to philanthropic pleadings is like sifting social invitations: You cannot expect all invitations to be enticing, and you need not be angry about those that aren't.

Of course, not all philanthropic overtures deserve tolerance. A healthy skepticism is required to eliminate the occasional frauds, or to deal with high-pressure telephone solicitations, or simply to weed out pleasant-sounding organizations that might not use your contribution efficiently. But the vast majority of personal requests will come from well-meaning people who represent excellent causes. While some solicitations do not require a formal refusal (for example, many mass fund-raising appeals), there are kind ways to handle the more personal, deserving solicitations that you need to turn down. A simple note or call can acknowledge that your philanthropic interests, at least for the moment, lie elsewhere.

The main thing is to respect worthy causes and to develop patience and appreciation for the people who are expending their time and effort (and probably their money as well) to improve conditions. There is no reason to shoot the messenger because you aren't impressed by the message delivered or because you are busy or are already overcommitted. The messenger for nonprofits should normally be appreciated, even praised.

Remind yourself, too, exactly how much time receiving solicitations takes. A person may work ten hours a day, devote an hour or two every few days to tennis or golf, and then consider as a nuisance the half hour requested to consider philanthropy. Charitable giving too often becomes the marginal time that takes the gaff for a variety of interruptions or frustrations. Expecting others to accomplish what we can do, yet avoid and resent, is one attitude that seriously blocks progress in our great country.

We must begin to cultivate a positive regard for private-sector efforts to eradicate local or national problems. Ancient Roman and Greek societies prospered partly because citizens were assumed to have personal obligations to perform for the good of the whole. And the richer the citizen, the more society expected of him. Plato, Aristotle, Machiavelli, and philosophers throughout history have concluded that good government relies upon a caring, cooperative citizenry. The ultimate decline of these great civilizations came from imperialism, not from the cooperative nature of their internal societies. The Greek word *idiotes*, from which the English word *idiot* is derived, meant a "private person" who did not participate in the common good of the state.

A significant number of our citizens seem willing to make sacrifices for the good of the nation. Still, the demands of special-interest groups have taken us a long way from the "all for one, one for all" philosophy that made American democracy unique and so productive.* Returning to a more patriotic concern for our society as a whole is the start toward effective citizenship and our ultimate recovery. Without this, and without this understanding by our political representatives, we may never get there.

---

*The Institute for Policy Innovation reports that there were 365 paid lobbyists working the US Senate in 1960, while today there are over 40,000.

A Need to Alter the Definition of Charity

Although dictionary definitions of *charity* reflect the laudable, positive aspects of benevolence toward those in need or disfavor and include such synonyms as kindliness, consideration, and humanity, the word may have less favorable connotations to many people. In short, to some, charity may imply helping others who refuse to help themselves, or who are ungrateful, or who are impinging on society's well-being (or on that of potential contributors). Since human beings are not identical, some recipients of donated money or time are bound to fall into these negative categories. But certainly not a large percentage. As with many of life's decisions, emphasizing the positive is the most fruitful approach. And in the case of charity, it is important to think of your efforts as *providing opportunity*. Providing those who are less fortunate a chance is the philosophy to follow — a chance to feel productive, to earn a living, to attain a happiness from the opportunity to live in a positive environment. As an old expression goes: Give a man a fish, feed him for a day; teach him how to fish, feed him for a lifetime. Reminding ourselves that charity is sharing what is generally a small part of ourselves or our assets in order to provide opportunity to less fortunate human beings — perhaps neighbors or fellow citizens — is an attitude that will produce positive results for all involved.

Another reason for thinking optimistically about the rewards of philanthropy is spiritual in nature. The tenets of practically all major religions encourage benevolence. Buddha, Muhammad, Maimonides, Jesus Christ, and many others teach us the wisdom, importance, and, yes, joys of sharing.

And do not neglect the personal psychological lifts that can be produced through philanthropy, not the least of which is self-esteem. Most humans respond favorably to a sense of belonging and particularly to a feeling of self-worth. Helping others is a conduit to both. It is a proven constructive habit that elevates self-image and generates lasting happiness.

From these pinnacles, philanthropic motivation descends through countless thoughts to reach the shocking yet unfortunately realistic suggestion made by author Tom Wolfe in his best-seller *The*

Bonfire of the Vanities. Wolfe describes a meeting of a nonprofit's representative with a Reverend Bacon to audit how the former's contribution to a day-care center in Harlem has been spent. (There had been no trace of where it went.) The Reverend Bacon's response is that the money had not truly been donated with the intention of providing for the children involved. "No," he says, ". . . you're investing in something else. You're investing in steam control. And you're getting value for money." Bacon was referring to what might be called denial or self-protection — in this case, keeping a segment of society's deterioration out of personal sight, and perhaps restricting violence to its own pocketed area, far away from the contributors.

Between the spiritual and religious and the Tom Wolfe extremes is, of course, a broad middle ground. Charity can be viewed as a practical and rewarding way to produce significant "selfish" pleasures. We may indeed look to philanthropy for "pleasure for pleasure's sake."

Whether you have an interest in art, music, dance, education, the environment, health, or history, philanthropic organizations offer great opportunities. Nonprofits cover virtually every field of human endeavor and offer an opportunity to associate with others who share similar interests. Donating personal time can be rewarding, and a contribution of money can be a door opener to intellectual or social opportunities. Highly regarded professional investor and author Peter Lynch noted in a May 1993 *Worth* magazine article that "there's no job that's more rewarding than my own experience of working with charities." Benjamin Franklin wrote that he "always set a greater value on the character of a doer of good than on any other kind of reputation." And Franklin himself founded and supported schools, hospitals, homes for orphans and the aged, as well as countless other worthy projects.

Philanthropy can also add to the cohesiveness of personal relationships. Friendships, marriages, and family life can only improve from the common acceptance of sound values that true charity represents. Consider the impact that grandparents, parents, or aunts and uncles might have on younger generations. Gifts need not be substantial in size to impress the young. What better example for younger people to emulate? What better training for the "do unto others" philosophy that most parents teach? What better example to prove that your actions are consistent with your words? The fact is that a breakdown of "family" has occurred in many parts of American life. We all suffer as a result, because our communities are weakened as families falter. If parents think only of themselves, what else can we expect from their offspring? If proper examples are not practiced at home, how can we expect our teachers to succeed? And, of course, if families do not favor helping others, how can we expect political decisions that are for the good of the whole?

Involving Your Family in Philanthropy

Money can be a curse. It has destroyed many family relationships, and it requires delicate handling. Since philanthropy involves the use of money, it has to be handled delicately, too. How children are treated, how involved or uninvolved they should be in their parents' finances (including their philanthropy) is a book unto itself. Properly handled, however, philanthropy can be

- a great teacher of sound values;
- a cohesive element — a fine common interest — for a ladder of generations within a family, as it should be among those within each distinct generation;
- a practical tool that helps young people learn about business; and
- a psychological boost for people of all ages and of all income levels, including those of inherited wealth, who often suffer from low self-esteem and even guilt stemming from their receipt of money they haven't "earned."

If you think you need guidance, there are consultants who help givers isolate the most effective providers in specific areas of need, and there are others who specialize in individual and family involvement in philanthropy, or simply in the broad subject of "dealing with wealth." H. Peter Karoff's Boston-based "Philanthropic Initiative, Inc." offers a fine questionnaire that can be of real help. Karoff has combined his views with those of Bob Graham's Namaste Foundation to produce the following list of positive effects of philanthropy on a family's well-being:

- A reduction in the sense of separateness from the larger world that people of wealth often experience
- A view of money as a blessing that can benefit many people beyond the possessor's narrow family unit
- A greater sense of personal wealth and self-esteem
- Establishment of a family purpose and team spirit
- A forum for meaningful intergenerational communication
- Training in "letting go" for the older generations
- A forum for practicing family democracy and power sharing

In fact, the relationship between friends or between spouses, as well as between parents and children, can benefit from joint involvement in charitable giving. As with parental involvement, the right kind of philanthropy can instill joint feelings of nurturing and a sense of pride that can foster closeness and provide greater fulfillment and happiness.

The children of Walter and Elise Haas of San Francisco were beneficiaries of such exposure and proved that they had learned their "lessons" well. The senior Haas's wills called for portions of their estate to go to charity, with the rest to be divided among their sons, Walter Jr. and Peter, and their daughter, Rhoda (Goldman). Already deeply involved in philanthropy, the three of them requested that their segments of the estate also be directed to charity instead of to themselves — something they have never regretted and something that has brought great happiness to each of them, as well as to their community.

Ed Littlefield, former chairman of Utah Construction Company and a generous contributor to worthy causes, was shocked by the poor statistical correlation between published lists of the wealthiest individuals and lists of major donors to charitable endeavors. He further lamented that too many wealthy people fail to get the message that "it is more blessed to give than to receive." Littlefield pointed out the positives of giving, however, by stating that "the givers of the world . . . have a desire to give because the act of giving makes them feel good . . . [and brings] them a sense of satisfaction that they have helped make the world a better place." His conclusion was that generosity "is a reasonable rent paid for a sunny place on the planet." As a friend said to me one day: "The charities themselves should also be more positive in their solicitations. Instead of emphasizing that donors should give till it hurts, they should ask them to give till it feels good."

Businesses can foster family feelings, too. Rewarding volunteers, supporting local causes, and showing concern for others is good for company image and morale, boosts community spirit, and can even help with client and customer acceptance. Levi Strauss, Ben & Jerry's Ice Cream, and a host of other companies have benefited from a Reaching Out philosophy that has made a positive difference. The R. B. Pamplin Corporation of Portland, Oregon, contributes $10 million yearly as a result of their goal to contribute 10 percent of pretax profits. As father and son Robert B. Jr. and Sr. say, "Philanthropy should be fun."

Such pursuits do not have to be grandiose. Take, for example, a San Francisco effort called Christmas in April. This is a local effort in which businesses contribute money for supplies and materials and encourage staff volunteers to add some elbow grease to refurbish a designated place worthy of such support. The 1992 project was a combined senior citizen and child care facility in an economically disadvantaged part of town.

In addition to refurbishing the building, Christmas in April had joyful side effects. According to one of the volunteers, "It was like seeing a miracle occur before my very eyes. In only one day we converted a shabby, dirty place into a 'spiffy' and attractive surrounding." And a man whose spouse had also joined in the face-lifting commented that the two of them felt great rapport with their four fellow workers and were elated by their joint accomplishment. All six now share a bond they hadn't felt before; they became new friends. And all ultimately became financial contributors to Christmas in April and more dedicated givers in a variety of ways.

So it all starts with attitude. This is what we have to change. The Reaching Out approach provides a specific outlet that can initiate the sort of change so desperately needed. It serves as a practical example of sharing that will filter through our children and our institutions to strengthen our existence. It will positively affect family, educational and religious structures, even business philosophies, and in the end it will create the kind of communities that can lead this nation forward to better conditions and attitudes.

Even without mates or family, giving can be a source of great personal joy. A November 1991 *New York Times* article on Mrs. Brooke Astor and her hands-on approach to charitable giving in New York City is inspirational. The article described the eighty-nine-year-old as "a woman of firm ideas" whose "determination to spend all of her fortune before she dies . . . has transformed her into New York's unofficial First Lady." Having donated over $170 million from her foundation since 1959, it's no wonder Mrs. Astor was hailed as "an anchor of New York society and philanthropy." More important than the plaudits from others, however, is the vibrant, fulfilling life led by Mrs. Astor. How many elderly people, rich or poor, enjoy such a sense of satisfaction? How many can honestly say, as she did, that "I have a lot more life in me!"?

Granted, Mrs. Astor had substantial funds to share. Yet there are numerous small, deserving organizations that will derive enormous benefits from moderate contributions by people of more limited means. A woman I know gave birth to a child with a deformity. She came to me and asked whether it would be possible to raise money to start a local support organization for parents of such children. It turned out that only $500 was needed. Needless to say, the money was donated and the parents — and children — are benefiting from the work of the group.

A short time ago, San Francisco's nonprofit Pickle Family Circus, which had brought great pleasures to thousands of children every year, suffered financial problems. A newspaper article led me to make a phone call. For a few thousand dollars, it turned out, and with the help of a half dozen others, the institution could be guaranteed a future by ensuring the preservation of its invaluable props and equipment. This was a far more pleasurable expenditure than countless personal purchases — and it was certainly more meaningful than keeping the money where it was.

Recently, my wife Louise and I visited a small Russian-emigré training center that we had established. We were extremely

touched by what we saw: people with almost no material possessions, many of them facing a language barrier, enthusiastically
starting from scratch to make a new life for themselves. Most had
spent a lifetime enduring religious or social discrimination and
had been directly or indirectly persecuted through the deprivation
of normal opportunities.

Our tour took us first to the English class, where we managed to communicate with twenty or thirty people who were strug-
gling — yet mastering — a new and foreign language. I couldn't
help but wonder how I would get by if my future suddenly de-
pended on being reasonably proficient in Russian. Not very confi-
dently or comfortably, I concluded. Yet the smiles and efforts by
the students to converse and answer questions from us expressed
their high hopes for themselves and their families, as well as a
great appreciation for the simple opportunity to be in a society
where freedom prevails. Our next stops were at computer-training
sessions and what might be termed "social graces" or "American
behavior patterns" classes, where we again conversed with people
who had so much to learn, so many obstacles to overcome, and
who were trying so very hard.

We departed a short time later, still emotionally affected, and
suddenly a thought struck me: there I was, a person fortunate to
have received more than my share of accolades and capital, and
yet at that very minute I was experiencing a "high" as pleasurable
as almost anything I had ever felt. And each time Louise and I talk
about that center, we feel just as proud and elated. How lucky we
are to be a part of something so meaningful.

I often look to one of the great social philosophers of our age,
John W. Gardner, for incisive statements about values, attitudes,
and directions. Gardner captured the essence of the joy of giving
and the need for greater involvement in his 1991 centennial com-
mencement address at Stanford University.

> The puzzle of why some men and women go to seed while
> others remain vital all of their lives concerns me today. I'm
> talking about people who have stopped learning or growing
> or trying . . . men and women functioning far below the
> level of their possibilities. I could without any trouble

name a half-dozen national figures resident in Washington, whom you would recognize, and tell you roughly the year their clock stopped.

You can keep the zest until the day you die. If I may offer you a simple maxim, "Be interested." Everyone wants to be interesting, but the vitalizing thing is to be interested. Keep your curiosity, your sense of wonder. Discover new things. Care. Risk. Reach out.

Chapter 5

Proving It Can Be Done

IT'S time to document more specifically whether the people in this country really are so conservative in their charitable giving and how much room there is for improvement. What do the data show?

In 1989 the Gallup Organization conducted a survey of the giving habits of people, including those in tax brackets of over $100,000 annual income. Some 25 percent of all persons surveyed admitted to being noncontributors. Interestingly, there was surprisingly little difference in the percentages of income allotted for charity among the giving groups. Other than those in the lowest income level (under $10,000), who indicated they donated at least 5 percent (perhaps owing to religious contributions), the respondents gave only between 2 and 3 percent. There was essentially no increase as income grew, and if it is assumed that those in the top bracket (which was listed as "$100,000+") might conservatively have averaged $125,000 in income, their resulting 2.3 percent giving was near the low end of the scale. The bottom line was that the poorest members of our population were proportionately the most generous.

While this survey provided some insight, it was only an entry point. I knew I had to find more precise statistics from much larger and more representative samples. Startling information came from analyzing the latest available detailed IRS data — the Preliminary

Table 1: Income and Charitable Contributions Filings, 1991

1	2	3	4	5	6
Total Adjusted Gross Income (AGI) Bracket	Average AGI per Return Including Capital Gains	Average AGI per Return Excluding Capital Gains	Average Charitable Contribution per Return Filed (Actual)	Contribution as a Percentage of Average AGI Including Capital Gains	Contribution as a Percentage of Average AGI Excluding Capital Gains
$ 25,000–50,000	$ 35,800	$ 35,500	$ 500	1.4	1.4
50,000–75,000	60,200	59,500	1,200	2.0	2.0
75,000–100,000	85,400	83,500	2,000	2.3	2.4
100,000–200,000	130,300	125,000	3,200	2.4	2.6
200,000–500,000	290,000	265,000	7,000	2.4	2.6
500,000–1,000,000	671,000	590,000	18,000	2.7	3.1
Over $1,000,000	2,360,000	1,825,000	87,000	3.7	4.8

NOTE: All numbers here and throughout this book are rounded.

Individual Tax Return Data, 1991. While the absolute 1991 numbers are naturally different from earlier ones, the most important ratios to be discussed here are consistent with the four preceding years, from 1987 through 1990.

Table 1 presents important statistics about total income and charitable contributions for a wide range of 1991 earners.

Table 1 Discussed

If you count capital gains on top of income, there isn't much difference in donation levels among the first six taxpayer levels listed (see column 5), and the highest AGI group's giving isn't dramatically higher. Excluding capital gains (column 6), there is minor progression, but the average incomes (columns 2 and 3) of the top two highest income categories are many times greater than those of the other five. It is equally disturbing that the second-highest earning group contributes little more than those in the lowest categories, even though substantial differences in income exist.

As shocking as these IRS figures seem, they only corroborate some broader conclusions reached in a 1989 study. *The Variability of Charitable Giving by the Wealthy,* by Gerald Auten and Gabriel Rudney, found that "regular, habitual giving is not the standard . . . behavior among high-income people" and that "large proportions of high-income individuals give less than 1 percent of [their] income."

It must also be emphasized that the figures in columns 4 through 6 of Table 1 are pretax contributions: after tax savings, the giving levels of 2 to 5 percent amount to only 1.6 to 3.5 percent, based on 1991's approximate 20 to 30 percent marginal tax rates — certainly not large sacrifices, particularly for those who earn on average $80,000 to perhaps as high as $2.4 million.

Note that the highest income group earns between fifty-one and sixty-six times what the lowest group earns. And consider, too, that these are comparisons of income only. When we discuss the dramatic disparities of total wealth that favor the high-income people, the conclusions are even more shocking.

Granted, these may not be perfect comparisons. Low-bracket giving may be exaggerated, since standard IRS deductions are

often taken, and these may be on average higher than actual gifts
that would be reported under itemizing. On the other hand, the
highest income groups are far more likely to employ tax professionals to maximize their deductions. No matter how you slice it,
the overwhelming evidence suggests that the giving percentages of
high-end earners have not been even close to what they might
have been.

Assessing the type of giving by high-income groups further re-
inforces this conclusion. Although there is no way to calculate donation quality or impact, philanthropy from the wealthy might be
exaggerated by their more frequent contributions of gifts that are
less tangible than those donated by lower-income filers — gifts
that produce little or no cash to the donee, such as art, books, con-
servation easements, collections, and the like. Such gifts, while
well intended and useful, may do little to overcome the serious social problems faced by our country today.

But the real test of relative levels of generosity must include
other considerations. As stated, annual income is one thing, net
worth and other factors (such as retained income and wealth after
spending) are decidedly another. Sadly, these other considerations
have been studiously avoided for ages, which may be one reason
why more comfortable living and increased giving have often been
neglected. So, to reach our ultimate goal of proving true surplus of
capital, let's now proceed to investigate the factors that determine
who is capable of elevating their living or giving without strain or
risk and how much they can afford.

Chapter 6

Breakthrough 1: How Spending Patterns Affect the Ability to Save

THE relationship between income and spending is obviously not linear. While there are people who spend whatever they earn, regardless of amount, those with higher incomes normally spend a smaller percentage of their income than those with lower earnings. A family with $30,000 in annual income may have to spend 90 to 100 percent of earnings (or more than 100 percent) to live reasonably well, while someone with $300,000 in yearly income can get by on a much smaller percentage. And the person with receipts in the millions should have plenty more to spare.

Whenever spending grows more slowly than income, the result is an expanded pot of excess income that provides a greater opportunity to save. And, of course, the more money saved, the greater the likelihood that overall wealth will expand, as the unused income is reinvested. This adds further to the capability of those with the highest incomes to spend more or give more money away. This is true on an absolute dollar basis, and it is especially true on a relative scale. Take the examples from the preceding paragraph of one person with $300,000 annual income, ten times more than another person's $30,000. Allowing for both needs and reasonable luxuries, the $300,000 earner should be able to save, give, or spend more than ten times the amount of the $30,000 earner.

But how much more? In order to determine how much more

individuals at varying levels of income can afford to save, give, or spend, we need to approximate their normal spending patterns.

Solving the Mystery of Relative Spending

Quantifying consumer spending and isolating discretionary income for various personal earning levels poses serious problems. While the federal government issues occasional statistics on expenditures such as food, alcohol, housing, and other personal outlays, these figures are not derived from documented reports such as yearly income declarations and are decidedly less exact. Furthermore, the data are not available for annual income levels above approximately $125,000. Calculating the discretionary income that remains after expenses and taxes is also imprecise, both because of the inexact spending figures and because there is no clear definition of what constitutes a necessary outlay and what is a luxury: one person's luxury is often another's necessity. Changing tax rates and the ingenuity of earners to shelter income from taxation present additional problems in arriving at reliable conclusions. While studies on spending and surplus/residual income are available, their conclusions are confusing. Some defy the logic that *relative* savings or spending potentials should rise in line with income.

Despite these problems, it was essential to estimate spending behavior — especially for the higher wealth categories that constitute the logical source for greater generosity, either to themselves or to society. My approach, although not highly scientific either, was as follows: first, I assessed the incremental spending experiences depicted in several reports; and second, I used the patterns that appeared most logical as a base from which to extrapolate incremental spending for the higher annual income groups. While there was no intent to prescribe a fixed level of spending for anyone, this approach produced ranges that represent reasonable norms, or "practical maximums," for people with varying means and related living standards. Most important, the conclusions allowed me to project what seems to be a sensible allocation of expenses and a logical approximation of residual income for various groups. The conclusions about the high earners add a relatively unexplored dimension to the subject of affordable giving.

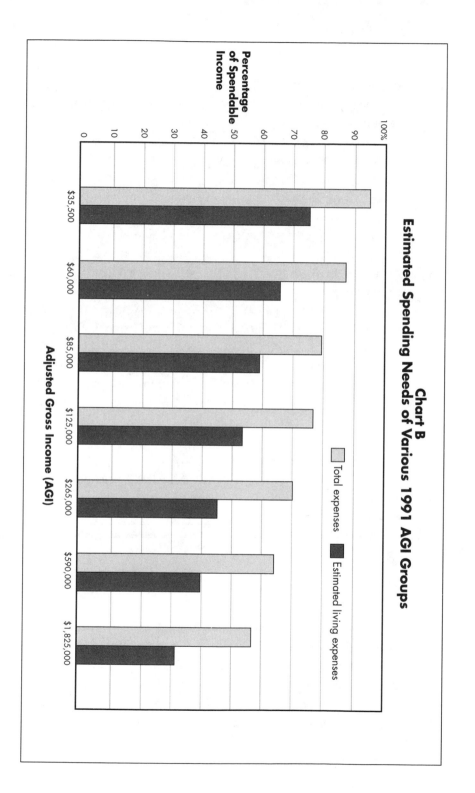

**Chart B
Estimated Spending Needs of Various 1991 AGI Groups**

Percentage
of Spendable
Income

100%
90
80
70
60
50
40
30
20
10
0

$35,500 $60,000 $85,000 $125,000 $265,000 $590,000 $1,825,000

Adjusted Gross Income (AGI)

☐ Total expenses   ■ Estimated living expenses

The results are shown in Table 2, which delineates how people do allow themselves extravagances as they become wealthier, but in proportionately decreasing amounts as their incomes (and assets) grow. Once people have covered their fixed costs and attained certain levels of luxury, they apparently either have little additional need to continue increased spending or they simply cannot find more things they will allow themselves to buy.

Table 2 Discussed

As column 3 indicates, the lowest income group's living expenses consume 76 percent of their spendable income, while the highest bracket group's outlays consume only 31 percent of theirs. Including all expenses and income taxes, column 5 shows that the two lowest earners have on average only 4 to 13 percent of their income left, while the highest have a healthy 36 to 43 percent left. Chart B displays these disparities.

Living expenses obviously vary dramatically from person to person, and almost any number will look inadequate if ostentatious consumption takes place. Still, I felt more confident with my allotments for the highest income groups after reading what a New York real estate developer received through a 1991 bankruptcy court filing. This individual claimed considerable extravagances and yet requested "only" $435,084 for six months' living expenses. Since that figure included $65,142 for staff salaries at his $6 million home, $74,034 for the crew of his $8.5 million yacht, $71,400 in maintenance fees for his primary residence, $62,898 for upkeep of another house, $30,348 for another boat, and $27,370 for insurance on a $7 million collection of vintage automobiles, you can see why Table 2's $560,000 figure for pretax spending should "work" for most of the highest-end earners.

I said earlier that the higher spending-to-income needs of lower- versus higher-income groups means that the $300,000 earner will be able to save, give, or spend more than ten times the amount of the $30,000 earner. And the one with receipts in the millions should have plenty more to spare. Now let's see if this is true, referring again to the highest and lowest earners listed in Table 2.

Table 2: Estimated Spending Needs of Various Adjusted Gross Income (AGI) Groups

	1	2	3	4	5	6
IRS Adjusted Gross Income (AGI) Category	Average Spendable Income (AGI)	Estimated Living Expenses[a]	Estimated Living Expenses as a Percentage of Spendable Income (AGI)	Estimated Total Expenses[b]	Total Expenses as a Percentage of Spendable Income (AGI)	Estimated Income Available for Savings
$ 25,000–50,000	$ 35,500	$ 27,000	76	$ 34,000	96	$ 1,500
50,000–75,000	60,000	39,000	65	52,000	87	8,000
75,000–100,000	85,000	49,000	58	67,000	79	18,000
100,000–200,000	125,000	66,000	53	95,000	76	30,000
200,000–500,000	265,000	120,000	45	186,000	70	79,000
500,000–1,000,000	590,000	232,000	39	379,000	64	211,000
Over $1,000,000	1,825,000	560,000	31	1,035,000	57	790,000

[a] Before taxes.

[b] Adding federal income taxes and Social Security taxes to living expenses; charitable donations not accounted for.

Using income alone, without adjustments for spending, the highest AGI (adjusted gross income) earner's $1,825,000 amounts to 51 times that of the lowest, $35,500 average earner. Accounting for spending, columns 5 and 6 indicate that the total expenses of the high-end group left $790,000 for potential savings, while the lowest group was left with $1,500. Dividing this $1,500 into the $790,000 of the high group would indicate that the wealthier people had 527 times as much saving power as the lowest-end earners. So an earning power that started out being 51 times higher becomes, after total expenses, 527 times higher than the surplus for the low-income group.

You can see how judging affordability by income alone is short-sighted and incomplete. You can also see the wisdom of giving greater weight instead to "residual income," which is my term for discretionary income after expenses or, more pertinent, income available for savings.

Thus, unless people with high incomes have exceptionally extravagant material desires or obligations, this relative spending/saving advantage is one reason that the odds favor the wealthy getting wealthier. And it is one reason to contend that there is significantly larger giving potential in the high-end groups than the traditional income figures, impressive though they be, suggest.

As convincing as this is, however, it generally pales in importance to asset ownership, the other definition of wealth, for which another significant breakthrough in our understanding is presented.

Chapter 7

Breakthrough 2: Adding the Critical Factor of Net Worth

AS we saw in Chapter 6, the relative saving power of different income groups is a crucial factor in determining affordability. But the more critical key to any definition of financial standing, adequacy, or, of course, affordability is net worth. To repeat, my definition of net worth includes net (after debt) earning assets and excludes nonearning holdings such as homes, possessions, and the like.

So the challenge was to quantify net worth, and I set out to find clues to the relationship between a person's income, which is reported annually to the IRS, and total wealth, which is normally hidden from view and not reported until after death. Death is the one time the government is privy to some official total wealth inputs. And for this there was information. The IRS had published studies of estate tax returns that had included total wealth data. But there were serious voids for my purposes. Unfortunately, the estate studies presented figures by income groups not compatible with later income data published by the same agency. Thus the data were not directly transferable to annual IRS income bulletins. In addition, estates represent people significantly older than the average of each year's IRS income compilations; also, it is safe to assume that maximum tax-saving efforts had already reduced asset values to a minimum as people approached their later years.

So I had to search elsewhere. But where? Hadn't net worth of living people divided into the IRS's regularly reported income groups been reported somewhere, sometime? Unfortunately, it hadn't; but it turned out that the IRS's regular "Statistics of Income" (SOI) reports served as an ideal source for this exact interpretation.

Sometimes the simplest approaches are the best, and it struck me that income reporting from individual tax returns might give reasonably precise clues to the market values of the majority of nonsalary income. To illustrate, if total taxpayers in the highest tax bracket reported dividend income of $1 billion for a year in which the Standard & Poor 500 Stock Index yielded 3 percent, dividing that $1 billion by 0.03 (to account for the 3 percent average return) would signify a $33.3 billion stock ownership value. Dividing this figure by the number of taxpayers who had filed would result in the average market value of common stock per filer. A simple and obvious solution.

I took the same approach to arrive at the value of bonds and other fixed-income instruments. The prevailing interest rates for the year in which income was reported were used to compute presumed market values. For example, if taxable interest rates were producing an average 7 percent yield, dividing the reported dollar interest income by 0.07 (for the 7 percent yield) resulted in the total estimated bond asset size. Again this was broken down by average amount per tax filer. The same procedure could be used for savings account and tax-exempt interest, mortgage income, and certain real estate income. While there were several other categories that required pure guesswork, they constituted a minority. Combining these extrapolated totals resulted in a fresh and documentable model for estimating net worth.

Later on, I learned that the Federal Reserve Board, the Treasury Department, the Census Bureau, and the IRS had made numerous efforts (some surveys, some based on reported figures) to ascertain wealth — and that an income capitalization method had been utilized in certain studies. None that I could find used the IRS Individual Income Tax Return Data groupings that can be followed year by year. Nor could I find any published text on the specific subjects of affordability or donation generosity emphasized here based on income capitalization. Finally, published studies concentrated mainly on total wealth, whereas my concentration was on earning assets.

This is not to imply that capitalization of income data is the best way to approach all analyses. The technique permitted me to attain what I considered practical: calculated averages for the various income groups. I also knew that the IRS annual income data are not totally reflective of reality because reported incomes are understated.* Still, the resulting net worth numbers were definitely adequate, and their understatement fit my demand that they be conservatively, not aggressively, estimated so that my conclusions would be similarly understated.

Although IRS-reported estate filings had not constituted an ideal source, they did provide a base for comparison with my conclusions. These cross-checks concluded that the estate values of comparable broad wealth categories were actually higher than the net worth calculations from my methodology described above. I chose the lower figures from my calculations because they dealt realistically with the ages of living people and because this approach allowed the conversion of any past or future income figures into comparable net worth numbers. Again, I used the lower, new calculations in order to be sure that recommended living and giving potential would be based on very conservative assumptions.

A Specific Example

Although an array of income and net worth groups will be covered here, the logical initial focus remains centered on the people of highest wealth. These include the 51,555 taxpayers in the highest IRS bracket (over $1 million AGI), where the preliminary 1991 average total income per return was $2.35 million inclusive of capital gains and $1.825 million without. Table 3 shows how earning-asset wealth, exclusive of personal possessions that produce no income, has been estimated through the capitalization of

---

*Bryant Robey, author of *The American People*, states that "almost one-quarter of all households say they earn money they do not normally report on their income tax returns."

Table 3: Estimated Earning Assets of 1991's Highest Average AGI Group

	1	2
Asset	*Actual 1991 Pretax Income*	*Estimated Asset Values*
Salaries and wages	$ 715,000	None
Bonds		
Taxable interest	245,000	3,700,000[a]
Tax-Exempt interest	95,000	1,650,000[b]
Common stock dividends	180,000	7,150,000[c]
Partnerships, Subchapter S corporations	485,000	2,400,000[d]
Business/professional income	70,000	200,000[e]
Rentals/royalties	35,000	900,000[f]
Miscellaneous	20,000	250,000[g]
TOTALS BEFORE DEBTS	$1,845,000	$16,250,000
Less interest paid on debts	20,000	250,000[h]
TOTALS AFTER DEBTS	$1,825,000	$16,000,000

[a] Based on weighted 1991 average yield of 6.6 percent.
[b] Based on weighted 1991 average yield of 5.7 percent.
[c] Based on 1991 Standard & Poor 500 Stock Index average dividend yield of 2.5 percent.
[d] Valuation based on five times reported income.
[e] Valuation based on three times reported income.
[f] Based on assumption that depreciation, operating expenses, mortgage interest, and other charges reduced reported earnings to approximately 4 percent of market value.
[g] Includes mainly estate/trust income assumed to yield 8 percent.
[h] Assumes 33 percent of debt ($20,000) is assigned to earning assets with averaged interest paid at 8 percent annually. Another debt of $500,000 is assumed to be against home(s) or similar non-earnings assets not included above; interest costs of $40,000 and principal repayments are paid from other income, also not shown above.

reported 1991 AGI. Column 1 shows rounded IRS figures and column 2 presents the rounded asset-value calculations based on the assumptions indicated in the footnotes.

While the calculations rely on certain assumptions, they are neither exorbitant nor wild guesses. The only real unknowns were on the 23 percent of earning assets represented by partnership and business/professional income and rentals/royalties and miscellaneous, all of which were accorded conservative treatment.

The bottom line of Table 3, column 2, indicates that the average person in this "over $1 million AGI" category thus had a rounded $16 million in conservatively valued earning assets.

Discovering Some Startling Facts

Calculating earning-asset wealth for this group and the next six AGI categories produced another breakthrough: an ability to answer the question "Which income groups had the highest *proportionate* net worth?" Logic suggested that those with the highest incomes had accumulated more assets, and substantially more on a comparative basis as income grew, but the challenge was to quantify the differences.

Using detailed IRS income sources and tax deductions from 1991, and following the procedures just described to arrive at the value of earning assets, I determined that the assumptions proved true. Table 4 shows conclusively that the ratio between productive, earning assets (exclusive of homes, possessions, and so on) and AGI is far more favorable for persons in the higher income brackets than for lower earners.

Table 4 Discussed

Column 2 shows the rounded earning-asset totals estimated for seven IRS income categories. And column 3 indicates the ratio of these assets to reported income. As that column shows, the two lowest-earning groups possess investments of little more than one year's total income (1.24 and 1.33 times, respectively); as expected, those groups depend more heavily on wages, salaries, Social Security income, and pensions. On the other end of the spectrum, with more income from investments in the hands of the higher earners, the highest two income brackets own investments 6.10 and 8.77 times one year's "pay." That's about five to seven times the relative wealth per dollar of reported income (excluding capital gains) for the highest two groups versus the lowest two.

More important, column 2 shows the highest income group's $16.0 million in assets, an amount 364 times the lowest income category's $44,000. Breakthrough 2 thus provides an efficient

Table 4: Estimated Earnings Assets Owned by 1991 IRS AGI Groups

1	2	3
Average AGI per Return Excluding Capital Gains	Estimated Income-Producing Assets	Ratio of Estimated Earning Assets to Reported AGI Excluding Capital Gains
$ 35,500	$ 44,000	1.24
60,000	80,000	1.33
85,000	150,000	1.76
125,000	400,000	3.20
265,000	1,300,000	4.91
590,000	3,600,000	6.10
1,825,000	16,000,000	8.77

barometer of what could be called "the net worth gap" — the huge disparity between the relative wealth of the high end versus other levels.

Net Worth and Giving

Just as these figures prove how much more asset ownership belongs to the highest earners, it seems indisputable that the combination of their higher income and significantly larger earning assets could have led to well-above-average giving, a generosity that the earlier figures showed is not the case.

Chart C compares relative giving to the relative assets owned by the seven income groups. The taller, light-colored bars, which measure the ratio of earning assets to AGI, show how much more wealth exists within the high brackets versus the low. And the small dark bars to their right show how little difference there is in the relative giving of the high versus the low earners.

Further Proof of the Potential for Greater Giving by the High End

As convincing as the statistics presented are, I decided to seek additional help, to analyze giving tendencies and determine both relative affordability and the ultimate giving patterns of different income and wealth groups. Dr. Jeffrey Moore and Tim Wei of Stan-

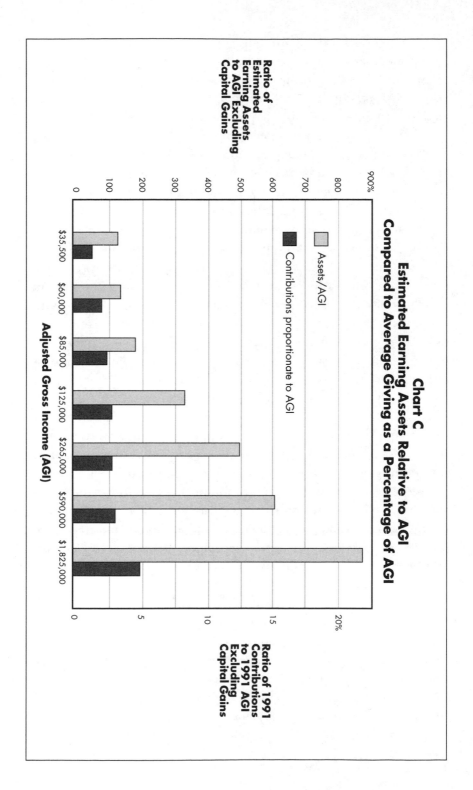

Chart C
Estimated Earning Assets Relative to AGI
Compared to Average Giving as a Percentage of AGI

Ratio of
Estimated
Earning Assets
to AGI Excluding
Capital Gains

Ratio of 1991
Contributions
to 1991 AGI
Excluding
Capital Gains

☐ Assets/AGI

■ Contributions proportionate to AGI

900%
800
700
600
500
400
300
200
100
0

20%
15
10
5
0

$35,500 $60,000 $85,000 $125,000 $265,000 $590,000 $1,825,000

Adjusted Gross Income (AGI)

ford's Graduate School of Business, ran numerous nonlinear statistical regression models that correlated sufficiently to prove the surprising, unexpected charitable-giving behavior of low versus high income/wealth groups. Two graphs in particular are worth reproducing here, the first of which, Chart D, plots 1991 contributions before and after tax deductions as a percentage of earning assets.

Charts D and E Discussed

As shown in Chart D, those 1991 taxpayers whose average earning assets (EA) were $400,000 or less — see the four blocks (squares) at the left portion of the chart — contributed between 0.8 and 1.5 percent of their EA to charity, while those in the higher brackets (average EA from $1.3 million on up, as shown by the bottom three blocks) contributed only about 0.4 percent. The four circles to the left show the after-tax costs of the lower four groups. Their donations ran from just under 0.6 percent to around 1.1 percent of EA, compared to an average of about 0.4 percent for the three in the higher wealth category. On an after-tax basis, those in the highest categories contributed one-third to two-thirds of what the lower income groups did as a percentage of wealth — even though the capacity of the high end was far greater than proportional and could have been many times the low end. Had those in the highest bracket been only as generous as the lowest two categories, their annual donations should have been two to three times the actual $87,000 from the IRS data.

Since one might argue that this discrepancy can be attributed to the significantly lower EA accumulated by the lowest groups, a test was made to compare the contributions as a percentage of residual income (or "Estimated Income Available for Savings," as in Table 2, column 6) to residual income itself. See Chart E.

The "resting hockey stick" curve in Chart E differs only slightly from the one in Chart D, so the depictions tell a similar story. Notice how the $1.825 million AGI group's approximate 10 percent contribution from residual income (at the far right) was either about the same or lower than the other six income categories. As in Chart D, the highest three AGI groups made lower relative charitable contributions than the lowest earners.

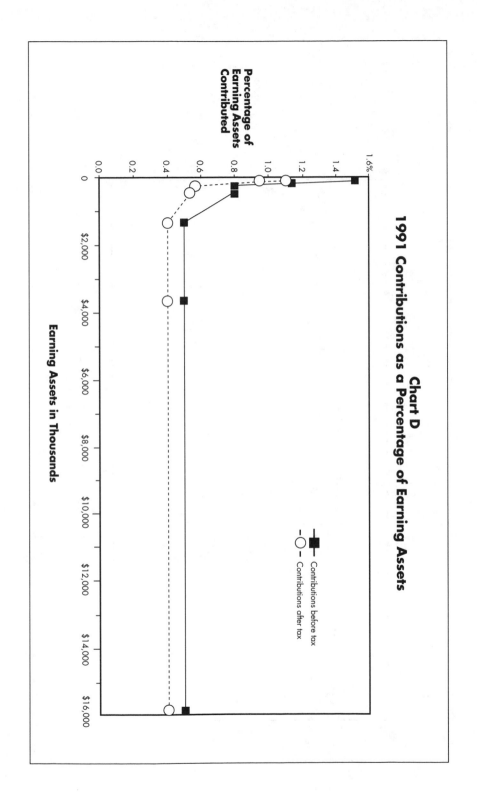

Chart D
1991 Contributions as a Percentage of Earning Assets

Percentage of Earning Assets Contributed

1.6%
1.4
1.2
1.0
0.8
0.6
0.4
0.2
0.0

0   $2,000 $4,000 $6,000 $8,000 $10,000 $12,000 $14,000 $16,000

Earning Assets in Thousands

■— Contributions before tax
○— Contributions after tax

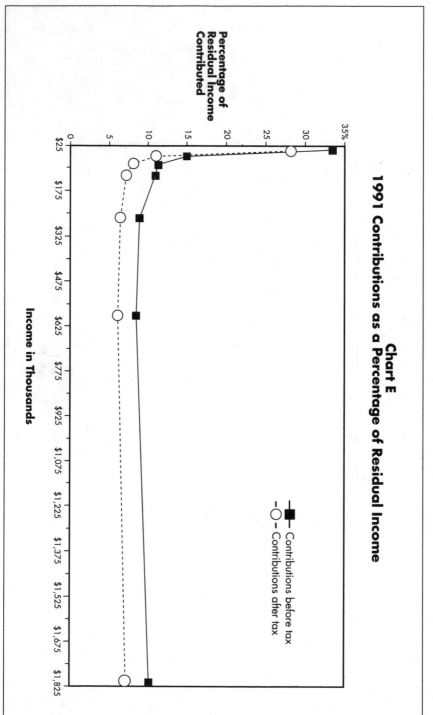

Chart E
1991 Contributions as a Percentage of Residual Income

Percentage of
Residual Income
Contributed

Income in Thousands

■ Contributions before tax
–○– Contributions after tax

These conclusions further confirm that significant potential for greater giving exists and that individuals simply have not developed their philanthropy as their wealth has grown. A newspaper article suggesting that churches should encourage more 10 percent tithing produced a joke that reflected this sad truth. The story related how a congregant had told his pastor he had no problem giving 10 percent of his income to the church when he made $50 a week, or even when he made $500 a week, but he was reluctant to do so when he made $5,000. In response "the pastor began to pray: 'Dear God, please make this man's income $500 a week so he can tithe.'"

The gap between the relative wealth of the high end and the lower brackets is where the greatest problem and the greatest potential for improvement in living and giving exist. The challenge is to raise giving enough to help society without endangering the reasonable financial security and bequest desires of the high-end groups.

Conclusions drawn from the tables and charts in this chapter might be suspect if the lower-income groups had suddenly gained a sharply higher share of the nation's affluence and quickly and generously converted it to donations while those in the highest brackets experienced asset declines and were suddenly frightened into a paucity of philanthropy. But such was not the case. The year 1991 was a bonanza period for investors in common stocks, with the S&P 500 Stock Index returning over 30 percent, and this positive result followed a 1987–1990 average return of approximately 12 percent per year. While real estate prices were lower, prosperity generally prevailed for the high end, which had benefited from the combination of high investment returns in the 1980s and a marginal tax rate reduction from a peak of 70 percent down to 28 percent. An explosion took place in the number of American millionaires, megamillionaires, and billionaires during this period.

The Forbes list of the four hundred richest Americans documents that this group more than tripled its wealth from $92 billion in 1982 to $328 billion in 1993. That's a compound annual growth of 12.3 percent per year, while inflation averaged but 4.2 percent each year over the same span. Yet you will recall that the 1980–1991 period found the average charitable donation from the top earners to have dropped by more than half.

By comparison, the median US family income barely exceeded the 1980–1992 cost-of-living increases. This is not to belittle the possibilities for enhanced giving by lower-income groups. While affordable increases pale compared to the high end, those in some lower-income and lower-personal-wealth categories, as well as corporations and even tax-exempt entities such as foundations, can add to the pot, too (as will be discussed). But Breakthrough 2 reveals that there is a large, virtually untapped resource in our country's high-end personal income and asset ownership groups. When the relative wealth figures of Breakthrough 2 are combined with the relative residual-income comparisons of Breakthrough 1, the conclusion is overwhelming: top bracket groups can easily afford to donate far more than they are, even while living more comfortably.

Chapter 8

Breakthrough 3: Identifying Your Financial Surplus

Introducing JASS — A Method for Judging Affordable Spending Sensibly

THE sports expression "two hands for beginners" implies that catching a ball is more assured when a player uses both hands rather than one. And there's a broader adage that applies to an endless number of human challenges: Two heads are better than one.

I hope that you now agree that the two criteria of income and net worth are also far superior to one in judging affordability, and that it is important to break the common habit of concentrating solely on income. *Money is money, it knows not its source, and it knows not the difference between a dollar of leftover income and a dollar representing an EA.* In fact, unless it's simply wasted by stuffing it into a mattress, a dollar of surplus income automatically becomes an EA that may become either more or less productive than the existing invested capital. Hence, *it's safe to say that a dollar already working as an EA is on average no more dangerous to part with than a dollar of surplus income.*

How then to proceed in the search for excess money that will allow you to achieve your spending goals and still feel safe in the process? How should you allocate proposed expenditures such as living better, making gifts to children, contributing to charities, and so on? And how should these allocations be compared to the two major financial sources of income and EA wealth?

I alluded to the wisdom of a dividing process in Chapter 1 when I reported that the 1991 top IRS income group's average pretax charitable donation amounted to 4.8 percent of its income with zero allocated to net worth; or reversed, to one-half of 1 percent of net worth with zero allocated to income. While these divisions showed how conservative the giving was, there is a better way to assess affordability for the vast variety of income and EA levels.

This realization led to "JASS," Breakthrough 3's system for Judging Affordable Spending Sensibly. JASS converts the myopic habit of concentrating on income alone to an understanding of the impact that any spending has on your *total* financial health.

There are two JASS approaches designed to benefit you. The first, labeled "Simplified JASS," is for those who are satisfied to gauge their affordability potential in an approximate way. And the second, labeled the "Detailed JASS" system, is for those desiring a more accurate picture of their finances. Since both approaches are easy to complete, you may want to use both.

To illustrate, let's use the 1991 average top bracket filer with $1.825 million in ordinary income and $16 million in EA. The Simplified JASS method will serve as the example to assess the actual $87,000 1991 donation, followed by Detailed JASS for the suggested more generous, yet, as you will see, affordable, $900,000 gift.

Case 1: Assessing the 1991 Charitable Donation of $87,000 (Rounded to $90,000), Using the Simplified JASS System

The goal: To compare the Simplified JASS approach to the pre-JASS habit of comparing the donation solely to AGI — that is, $90,000/$1,825,000 = 0.048, or 4.8% of AGI.

The Simplified JASS System:

Step 1. Deduct this bracket's donation tax saving of 40 percent, leaving 60 percent of $90,000 = a $54,000 after-tax donation.

Step 2. Divide the $54,000 into two equal parts = $27,000 each.

Step 3. Divide the first $27,000 by the $1,825,000 AGI = 0.0148, or a rounded 1.5 percent of the year's income.

Step 4. Divide the second $27,000 by EA of $16,000,000 = 0.0017, of seventeen-hundredths of 1 percent of EA.

Probable Conclusion: You can see how small the actual 1991 donation was. After tax savings, it amounted to 1.5 percent of income and less than two-tenths of 1 percent of EA. Assuming the

1.5 percent doesn't convert surplus income to a deficit, the two-tenths of 1 percent of EA means that the same $90,000 donation could be duplicated for five years before there is even a tiny 1 percent reduction of the $16 million EA. And remember that no allowance has been made for any capital appreciation from existing EAs. So you can see how the added information from this simplified JASS system is far superior to the habit of considering the donation as solely, in this case, 5 percent of income.

Simplified JASS provides additional insights when splitting percentages are changed. For example, instead of a 50-50 split, allocating two-thirds of the $54,000 to income and one-third to EA alters the ratios to 2 percent of AGI and just over one-tenth of 1 percent of EA — hence, if the 2 percent doesn't convert surplus income to a deficit, the donation might persist for ten years before reducing EA by 1 percent. Let's proceed now to a contemplated $900,000 donation, this time using the Detailed JASS approach:

Case 2: Assessing a More Generous Charitable Donation of $900,000, Using the Detailed JASS System

The goal: To compare the Detailed JASS approach to the pre-JASS accepted usage of comparing the contemplated donation solely to AGI — that is, $900,000 / $1,825,000 = 0.48, or 48% of AGI, most probably a frightening prospect for most people.

The Detailed JASS System:

Step 1. Deduct tax savings of 40 percent, leaving 60 percent of $900,000 = a $540,000 after-tax donation.

Step 2. Deduct your expected living and other expenses, including taxes, from your AGI. Using Table 2, see column 6 of page 53 = $790,000. This is your surplus/discretionary income.

Step 3. Calculate what portion of EA this surplus income amounts to: $790,000 divided by $16,000,000 = 0.049, or a 4.9 percent addition to EA.

Step 4. Now calculate what percentage of EA the contemplated $540,000 after-tax donation represents. Divide $540,000 by $16,000,000 = 0.034, or 3.4 percent of EA.

Step 5. Subtract Step 4's 3.4 percent reduction from Step

3's 4.9 percent addition to EA, leaving a positive of 1.5
   percent of EA. This is the net effect on total EA
   wealth brought about by the contemplated donation.
Step 6. Factor for whatever capital appreciation or depreciation you might logically expect from your EA over
   the years (see below). While nobody should expect precision from such estimates, neither should the consideration be ignored.

Probable Conclusion: Despite the $900,000 donation, EA has
grown by 1.5 percent, not bad for a person of this wealth — especially since no allowance has been made for any increments in
value of the EA over time. If, for example, half of the $16 million
EA consists of common stocks that might be expected to grow an
average of 6 percent per year, the 3 percent net increment to Step
5's 1.5 percent leaves a net positive 4.5 percent of EA. With or
without assumptions on possible changes in EA values, the JASS
tests of affordability are vastly superior to the existing narrow
scope that arbitrarily concludes that the higher $900,000 donation
is imprudent because it amounts to almost 50 percent of AGI.

Two other comments. First, whereas the conversion of spending potentials from pretax to posttax should be applied consistently, Simplified JASS's splitting-of-wealth technique works best
when AGI and EA are reasonably well balanced. If either one is
outsized relative to the other, ratios computed on the smaller com-
ponent may appear overwhelming and discourage what may be
very affordable spending opportunities. Second, there is no one
percentage conclusion that works for everyone — age, legacy
plans, health factors, insurance coverage, and other factors must
also be considered.

Still, Detailed JASS provides the necessary basics, and both
JASS approaches are convenient, simple measures of affordability
potentials that should open new vistas into the subject of personal
finances. These, along with other *Wealthy and Wise* inputs, provide a necessary new definition of philanthropic affordability. Just
as you shouldn't focus solely on the oil pressure and ignore the gas
gauge of your automobile, the JASS formats should aid in eliminating the old, truly outmoded habit of relating spending to income
alone.

Chapter 9

Breakthrough 4: A Lifelong Financial Statement

HISTORICALLY, efforts to encourage more generous giving have concentrated either on the incomplete and potentially deceptive element of income alone or on personal satisfaction, need, and morality. This book covers some of the latter factors, but the emphasis centers on a careful, measured approach to assured, tangible financial matters. The joys of giving are important, but the impetus to greater joy must come from an increased confidence that such generosity is affordable.

Forty years of investment experience have produced in me a deep respect for financial conservatism, a recognition of the inevitability of economic and investment cycles, a respect for protecting against inflation, and a firsthand view of the traumas that lower net wealth can create. The challenge then was to convert this experience into numbers that would prove conclusively that enlightened giving and more relaxed living can be practiced. Breakthrough 4 accomplishes this — and more. This breakthrough is based on a series of computer-generated financial programs that provide space for a normal living budget, an investment portfolio with suggested average rates of return, taxes, intended bequests at death, and suggested allocations for charitable giving. The end result of these programs is to provide people interested in understanding their present and future wherewithal with a way to estimate year-by-year their average wealth — over one-, five-, ten-, twenty-, and thirty-year spans. Figures are expressed both in nominal dollar terms and in "real" terms that adjust for inflation at 3 percent annually.

Breakthrough 4 is what investment expert Charles Ellis of Greenwich Associates labeled a "lifelong financial statement." Ellis wrote to me: "You have shown people how to combine future incomes and capital appreciation that can be incorporated into a present plan for the future. You have defined both the affordable dollar amounts and the duration of their focus that might be ever-so-safely practiced."

That certainty has been my intent. After all, no one should dissipate security by spending too much on giving or higher standards of living, or even by striving too quickly toward these goals.

Not that this has been the problem. Quite the contrary. Charitable giving has played little or no role in the vast majority of occurrences of such depletion. In fact, I've never heard of a case where the culprit was philanthropy. Sadly, depletion has often occurred through events quite different from the responsible financial planning that is being proposed here.

How Breakthrough 4 Works

Table 5 on pages 74–75, a Projection of Finances Worksheet, is important for its practicality, and it is especially useful because it includes the two elements of income and earning-asset value that are critical to so many financial judgments and conclusions. The table contains data for 1991's highest average AGI ($1.825 million) earning group, but to be conservative and more current, the higher tax rates existing in 1994 have been added. Further conservatism was used in setting the tax *moderately* below the highest marginal rate of 39.6%, despite the fact that most taxpayers find enough shelters to pull their average rate *well* below the maximum level; in addition, the 1991 estimated living expense was raised to $590,000 (from $560,000) to adjust for inflation.

Table 5a is a blank version of Table 5 for your use. The white squares with asterisks indicate the most likely items to be identified and factored for conclusions.

Let's start with a one-year compilation that covers both the

AGI and EA figures but separates them for display purposes. This is a format that should be easily understood and used by anyone assessing his or her finances. For the Table 5 example, I have chosen the $16 million calculated EA ownership explained in Chapter 7; this represents a single person or a married couple — it fits both categories. Obviously, the reporting entity is doing very well.

The first portion of Table 5 deals with salary, wages, and other income not emanating from earning assets. IRS data show that around $715,000 of the $1,825,000 reported income (after deducting interest charges) came from such salary-type sources, while the remaining $1,110,000 was derived from EAs held in a diversified portfolio of savings accounts, bonds, common stocks, real estate, partnerships, Subchapter-S corporate and other business and professional income (see page 58).

Following the salary category is the section on fixed-income earning assets — cash investments and bonds (mortgages owned might belong here too). Column 1 lists the market value of these fixed-income securities; columns 2 and 3 indicate the income and related taxes incurred, culminating in column 4, the net income after taxes. The next three columns plot how the capital gains and associated taxes would have looked had the investments been sold. In the case of our example, no fixed-income holdings were sold, so the $5.35 million in column 9 is identical to column 1's initial value. This is fairly typical, for such investments are usually (but not always) held for their long-term income benefits.

Next, we add the year-end results of equity investments to this same table. These investments, mainly the common stocks and real estate holdings, fluctuate in their market values and have the greatest potential for growth and profit (or loss); stocks are normally traded or sold more often than real estate or fixed-income assets. The "Other" category includes business/professional ownership positions. For the purposes of our example, 6.0 percent of the $10.9 million, or $651,000 (see column 5) represented an increase in value of those holdings during that year, while the $429,000 in column 6 was realized (this is the portion of the $10.9 million that was sold; it might have been larger but for the use of appreciated securities allocated for donations). Column 7 shows the $129,000 tax on this realized capital gain. The

Table 5: Projection of Finances Worksheet

	Income Items			
	1	2	3	4
	Market Value of EA	Annual Income Excluding Capital Gains	Less Tax on Income	Net Income after Taxes
Salary and other non-asset-related income		715	254	461
EARNING ASSETS				
FIXED-INCOME INVESTMENTS				
Cash investments				
Taxable	2,200	128	45	82
Nontaxable	750	35	0	35
TOTAL CASH INVESTMENTS	2,950	162	45	117
Bond investments				
Taxable	1,500	119	42	76
Nontaxable	900	59	0	59
TOTAL BOND INVESTMENTS	2,400	178	42	135
Other	0	0	0	0
TOTAL FIXED-INCOME INVESTMENTS	5,350	340	87	252
EQUITY INVESTMENTS				
Common stocks	7,150	180	64	116
Real estate	900	35	9	26
Other	2,850	575	204	371
TOTAL EQUITY INVESTMENTS	10,900	790	277	513
a Gross totals	16,250	1,845	619	1,226
b Less debt, interest expense, and tax saving	(250)	(20)	7	(13)
c Gross totals after debt	16,000	1,825	612	1,213
d Deduct charitable donation of		(87)		
e Add tax saving from donation			34	
f Net effect of donation				(53)
g Net totals after taxes			577	1,161
h Less 32% living expenses				(590)
i Net cash flow from income				571
j Transfer surplus income to EA				(571)
k Net EA with surplus cash added				0
Recap of charitable gift donation Amount: 87		After-tax cost: 53		
(l) JASS even split of donation Assign to AGI: 44		Assign to AGI: 27		
(m) JASS donation as percentage of AGI: 2.41%		Percentage of AGI: 1.48%		

(all figures in thousands of dollars except %s as shown)

		Earning-Asset (EA) Items		
5	6	7	8	9
Estimated One-Year Unrealized Capital Gain	Estimated One-Year Realized Capital Gain	Less Estimated Tax on Realized Capital Gains	Changes in Market Values after Gains or Losses and after Tax Effects	EA Values after Market Price Changes
0	0	0	0	N.A.
0	0	0	0	2,200
0	0	0	0	750
0	0	0	0	2,950
0	0	0	0	1,500
0	0	0	0	900
0	0	0	0	2,400
0	0	0	0	0
0	0	0	0	5,350
501	286	86	415	7,565
36	0	0	36	936
114	143	43	71	2,921
651	429	129	522	11,422
651	429	129	522	16,772
				16,522
				571
				17,093

Assign remainder of after-tax cost to EA: 26
Remainder of after-tax cost percentage of EA: 0.0016%

Table 5A: Projection of Finances Worksheet

	Income Items			
	1	2	3	4
	Market Value of EA	Annual Income Excluding Capital Gains	Less Tax on Income	Net Income after Taxes
Salary and other non-asset-related income		*	*	*
EARNING ASSETS				
FIXED-INCOME INVESTMENTS				
Cash investments				
Taxable	*	*	*	*
Nontaxable	*	*	*	*
TOTAL CASH INVESTMENTS	*	*	*	*
Bond investments				
Taxable	*	*	*	*
Nontaxable	*	*	*	*
TOTAL BOND INVESTMENTS	*	*	*	*
Other	*	*	*	*
TOTAL FIXED-INCOME INVESTMENTS	*	*	*	*
EQUITY INVESTMENTS				
Common stocks	*	*	*	*
Real estate	*	*	*	*
Other	*	*	*	*
TOTAL EQUITY INVESTMENTS	*	*	*	*
a Gross totals	*	*	*	*
b Less debt, interest expense, and tax saving	*( )	*( )	*	*( )
c Gross totals after debt	*	*	*	*
d Deduct charitable donation of		*( )		
e Add tax saving from donation			*	
f Net effect of donation				*( )
g Net totals after taxes			*	*
h Less 32% living expenses				*( )
i Net cash flow from income				*
j Transfer surplus income to EA				*( )
k Net EA with surplus cash added				
Recap of charitable gift donation Amount: *			After-tax cost: *	
(l) JASS even split of donation Assign to AGI: *			Assign to AGI: *	
(m) JASS donation as percentage of AGI: *			Percentage of AGI: *	

		Earning-Asset (EA) Items		
5	6	7	8	9
Estimated One-Year Unrealized Capital Gain	Estimated One-Year Realized Capital Gain	Less Estimated Tax on Realized Capital Gains	Changes in Market Values after Gains or Losses and after Tax Effects	EA Values after Market Price Changes
*	*	*	*	*
*	*	*	*	*
*	*	*	*	*
*	*	*	*	*
*	*	*	*	*
*	*	*	*	*
*	*	*	*	*
*	*	*	*	*
*	*	*	*	*
*	*	*	*	*
*	*	*	*	*
*	*	*	*	*
*	*	*	*	*
				*
				*
				*

Assign remainder of after-tax cost to EA: *

Remainder of after-tax cost percentage of EA: *

$11.442 million in column 9 is the sum of the original $10.9 million plus column 5's $651,000 unrealized gain, minus the $129,000 in taxes listed in column 7.

The "Gross Totals" (line a of page 75) is a sum of the columns above it. Note that we have not yet added any of the income items to EA (the net effects of the pluses and minuses from income in column 4 will be transferred to EA at the end). Column 9, line a, indicates that EAs have risen to $16.772 million, as a result of the equity market value increases minus the taxes paid on realized capital gains. Line b subtracts the debt outstanding: the $250,000 in column 1 reduces column 9's EA to $16.522 and its $20,000 interest results in line c's AGI becoming $1.825 million (column 2). Lines d through g account for the $87,000 charitable donation. Line h then accounts for Table 2's living expense of $560,000, adjusted upward for inflation to $590,000, leaving row i's "Net Cash Flow from Income" as a positive of $571,000. In line j, this surplus is transferred to EA, and finally, in row k, column 9, the conclusion is that EA has grown to $17.093 million — a 6.8 percent increase over the original $16.000 million. Assuming inflation ran 3.0 percent in that year, this individual has seen his or her inflation-adjusted EA grow by 3.8 percent.

From this compilation, the taxpayer can estimate how much more or less might be spent on living expenses or other costs that will not affect taxation. And now we are also in a position to approximate what, if any, additional amounts might be contributed to charities, allowing of course for tax deductions to be received at the highest marginal rate.

A JASS reminder is presented at the bottom of the table. The $87,000 donation has been lowered to its after-tax cost of approximately $53,000, which is then split into $27,000 and $26,000 pots that are allocated separately to AGI and EA. The final line shows the calculated JASS donation percentages: 1.48 percent of AGI and 0.0016 percent of EA.

Let's assume now that this same high-wealth individual wants to make a large gift of, say, $813,000 more than the $87,000 she has already contributed. Testing the affordability of this starts with the EA conclusion of Table 5 and proceeds to account for the proposed new donation:

EA wealth from line k of Table 5, column 9	$17,093,000
Deduct proposed additional charitable donation	(813,000)
Add 39.6% tax saving from donation	322,000
Leaves EA of	$16,602,000

Can anyone really estimate accurately the future performance of earning assets as indicated in the tables? The answer is no, particularly over a term as short as one year. But no one should ignore the prospects for changes in values. You certainly wouldn't invest in common stocks yielding an average of only 2.5 percent unless you expected eventual capital appreciation. Nor would you buy certain properties or businesses without such hopes.

The longer the view of earning assets, the more reliable the forecasting of capital values is. Near-term volatility averages out over time, and history has shown that total returns (a combination of income and capital values) are far more consistent if looked at over five- and, most particularly, ten-year intervals.

The lifelong financial statement provides a structure for estimating financial wherewithal for short and long terms. As shown, it provides a compact way to assess any monetary surpluses or deficits that in turn should help you to decide what is reasonable to spend or donate. Additional information and thoughts will be provided throughout the balance of this book, with an approximation of what might be affordable for a myriad of income and net worth combinations. I will explain how you will be able to locate estimated spending potentials for any one, or a series, of such combinations.

The Final Matrix

The final matrix of Breakthrough 4 is a compilation of hundreds of one-year Table 5 formats for a vast number of income and earning-asset wealth levels. Concentration has centered on a series of five-year records of income and capital appreciation from various EAs, inflation, living expenses, taxes, and even plausible donations to charities. Consideration is also given to inheritance needs. The goal is simply to indicate in general what people of varying incomes and net worth might afford to give, along with the projected estimated effects such giving might have on future asset values. Are assets likely to grow or shrink from their initial values due to enhanced giving? And by how much? To respond to such questions, the matrix lists incomes ranging from as low as $35,500 all the way up to a staggering $100 million; earning assets range from one hundred dollars up to $500 million. Chart F, an illustration of the matrix, shows only one "cell" of the many that exist.

Chart F Discussed

Income groupings are listed horizontally across the top; the vertical column at left lists the earning-asset wealth. Nonearning assets have been excluded despite the fact that they can often be converted to earning power by the owners or their heirs. And not all nonearning assets are homes and possessions, either: real property such as bare land or stocks paying no dividends, or IRAs and pension funds, do not show up in these calculations, yet they can have sizable values. The matrix produces three figures for each combined income and asset level, as the illustration demonstrates.

The box in this example reflects a taxpayer with an income of $125,000 and earning assets of $400,000 who is considering a $9,000 donation. Assuming five years of giving at this level and then five more at a lower rate (assumed to be at the same ratio to AGI and EA that existed in the 1991 base year), the combination of investment returns, taxes, spending, and inflation produces an estimate that EA might reach roughly $527,000 at the end of year five and $703,000 at the conclusion of year ten. Hence, this person's starting total asset value has actually grown on an inflation-adjusted basis over the half-decade and decade time periods.

Needless to say, the matrix numbers are only approximations. While the various assumptions are logical and prudent, claiming specific accuracy would be irresponsible. But as guides to understanding ballpark amounts prudently available for philanthropy or for improved living standards, the examples are certainly superior to the "stab-in-the-dark" approach that has existed for aeons. The model and the related suggestions that are presented throughout this text place money into a better perspective. Absolute dollar amounts often tend to frighten people, especially without an

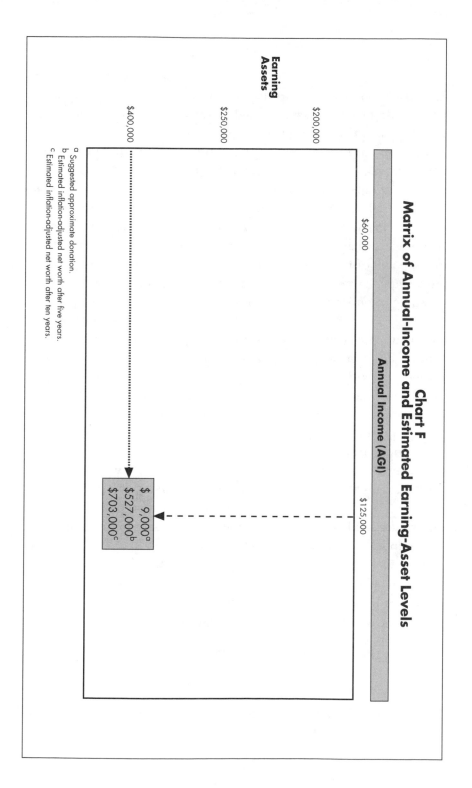

Chart F
Matrix of Annual-Income and Estimated Earning-Asset Levels

Annual Income (AGI)

	$60,000	$125,000

Earning Assets

$200,000

$250,000

$400,000

$ 9,000[a]
$527,000[b]
$703,000[c]

[a] Suggested approximate donation.
[b] Estimated inflation-adjusted net worth after five years.
[c] Estimated inflation-adjusted net worth after ten years.

awareness of their relative significance. Unnecessary fears can be mitigated through the thought process of Table 5 and the matrix examples.

Some Personal Examples

A friend of mine with sizable assets continued to give $5,000 to the same charity year after year. Time flew by, and one day my friend confessed to me that he hadn't adjusted that donation or any other for time, inflation, or his greatly increased asset wealth. So, using the process of Breakthrough 4, together we figured out what he could safely afford. It turned out to be five times the amount he had been giving in the past.

In a way, understanding affordability is like a game my wife and I repeat when we consider certain purchases. One day some years ago, Louise mentioned that she had seen a lovely dress but that it seemed "too expensive." Let's say the price was $100. My response was that a similarly priced item thirty or so years before probably would have been marked at a small fraction of $100. We quickly approximated the effects of thirty-plus years of inflation and determined the price in "good-old-days" terms to be around $10, at which moment my wife was quickly out the door on her way to you-know-where.

Well, other living costs — and certainly charitable giving — deserve the same mathematical common sense, which is basically what this fourth series of breakthroughs has produced. The charts, tables, and recommendations presented provide practical guidelines, including both current and future perspectives. As shown, any combination of wealth and income, as well as any chosen mix of earning assets, can be plotted to set giving levels that can (after allowing for tax deductions and inflation) be targeted for any given approximate *future* wealth goal. Again, precision is impossible, but order-of-magnitude projections are plausible — so that a person with "x" dollars of present assets can work backward from the chosen "y" wealth of the future to determine reasonably affordable giving for today.

Chapter 10

Breakthrough 5:
A Flexible Plan

MANY people develop conscious and unconscious barriers to charitable giving. While the amount of money to give is always a consideration, sometimes it's the fear of a long commitment that bothers people. Common sense suggested to me that flexibility must exist for anyone contemplating philanthropy, and the result were the breakthroughs of this chapter.

My initial thought on affordable giving was to suggest a logical ladder of financial commitment that shifts according to broad wealth levels of potential givers (see box).

Because lifetime commitments can be discouraging, I patterned

Broad Income/Net Worth Categories	General Planning/Thinking Suggested for Giving
"Very wealthy"	A lifetime commitment, with a definite plan for now and the future.
"Wealthy"	Possibly a lifetime commitment, possibly ten years, with a specific plan in mind for ten.
"Very comfortable"	Think in terms of a five-year plan.
"Reasonably comfortable"	Contemplate three to five years.
"Others with some cushion over their spending"	Start with a one- or two-year plan.

my models for increased giving to a maximum of five years. By doing so I hoped to expand the number of people to whom these worthy new habits will appeal. Again, greater flexibility is the plan, with five years used as a maximum "trial period" for the top wealth groups, and possibly less-than-five-year plans for lower-income and lower-net-worth givers. (Note: Multimillionaires and wealthier people can certainly think in philanthropic terms beyond five years — but the matrix compilations shift after five to 1991 contribution ratios.)

These conclusions were an extension of the caveat that people should reassess their circumstances regularly, whether they are reviewing their living standards or patterns of charitable giving. They also supported Breakthrough 4's spreadsheets, which were designed to produce (1) growing inflation-adjusted net worth for most people even after budgeting sharply heightened donations, and (2) substantial hikes in net worth for lower EA people wherever their AGI or EA gains will allow it, and similar increments for all categories after a return to normal giving beyond five years. It was important to show that ten-year projections looked very healthy, and that twenty- or thirty-year figures were robust enough to erase many of the potential worries of those who were not accustomed to generous giving. Finally, the five-year-or-less options encourage more groups to initiate giving strategies that offer positive opportunities for themselves, their families, their communities, and our nation.

This flexibility also helped erase another common hangup: the arbitrary maximum donation to a particular charity, which can hold back overall giving. Strange as it may sound, setting a dollar limit to one organization in a given year is possibly a stronger focus of most people than is their total giving.

What does this have to do with flexible time horizons for different donors? The answer is that piercing the "one-organization maximum-gift barrier," even if it entails just making a pledge for a second year, helps to raise the donor's comfort level for future specific gifts and his or her annual total, too. A person who has never given more than, say, $500 to one charity may eventually erase that limitation once a commitment has been made to contribute $1,000 over two years. This does happen! And, of course, once a $1,000 number becomes comfortable, the door is open to a larger total.

As mentioned, flexibility over time is very important. Consider two individuals with the same income but with different amounts of assets owned. Thinking in shorter horizons opens up the possibility that the one with larger net worth might consider a five-year plan, while the person with fewer assets might be attracted by a shorter, say, two-year, period. This ought to alleviate the problem that — even with constant reassessment — five years might simply seem too overwhelming to some. After all, this book is about personal, subjective levels of financial comfort and a respect for conservatism.

To summarize, individuals can "mix and match" components of the numerous breakthroughs over the course of their lives. As income, net worth, and spending needs change, enhanced giving can also change, with adjustments made in both the amounts and the duration of the gifts.

The Breakthroughs Recapped

Breakthrough 1. Concentrates on income and expense, showing approximate expenses for important tax brackets. Proves that people in the highest bracket have disproportionately more income available for saving (or spending or giving) than those in the lower brackets, and that the odds greatly favor the wealthy getting wealthier.

Breakthrough 2. Approximates net worth for the top seven tax brackets, thus adding the critical key to understanding financial adequacy or affordability. Proves the overwhelming relative net worth of the higher income groups versus the lower. Further proves the undergiving of the high bracket groups relative to EA and to residual income.

Breakthrough 3. Adds the new JASS (judging affordable spending sensibly) method to improve understanding of surplus funds by breaking anticipated spending amounts into two parts and then calculating what each part represents as a percentage of the two variables of income and EA. JASS suggests the use of after-tax figures for such calculations. Its overall approach provides psychological support for an improved understanding of financial affordability.

Breakthrough 4. Provides a "lifelong financial statement" that allows people to plot their financial wherewithal — present and potential — for extended periods of time. This allows for a greater sense of security in understanding what is truly affordable for better living or enhanced giving.

Breakthrough 5. Allows a flexible time frame for enhanced spending, thus alleviating anxieties over increased giving, whether from capital or income.

Chapter 11

Point/Counterpoint: Separating Rational and Less Rational Arguments For and Against Greater Giving

THE breakthroughs present new understandings of personal financial wherewithal. Despite the logic, resistance to financial proof may emanate from the complicated and, in some cases, irrational ways that people think about money. This chapter is designed to raise and then rebut some of the arguments commonly offered against greater giving and more comfortable living, arguments that often create barriers to a more fulfilled life.

To simplify, the arguments and responses have been divided into three categories: (1) concerns that might be removed through investment, insurance, tax planning, or other financial management approaches; (2) obstacles that might be overcome through good advice on how to give wisely; and (3) habits or emotions that, to be altered, may require more than the suggestions found in the first two categories.

Category 1: Arguments Refutable by Specific Investment, Tax Planning, or Other Approaches

Problem: Many people worry about preserving their current lifestyle and ensuring future minimum inheritances for children and family. Their insecurities also include a concern that they will live too long and that no sum is protection enough against rising living and medical costs that might be incurred. After all, inflation can erupt and eat away at purchasing power, and deflation or economic depression may sharply reduce income and asset values as well.

Solution: These insecurities range from highly proper concerns to great exaggerations. Although most people must remain conservative spenders, many people with vast amounts of wealth simply don't allow themselves the contentment of feeling secure. Yet their money could be spread broadly enough among diverse types of investment to protect their wealth against most any circumstance short of drastic, unprecedented "governmental actions" such as confiscation, financial system collapse, or natural disasters.

Diversifying into a variety of investment types is one solution, and using debt conservatively is another. Protecting inheritances can be accomplished through various trust forms and better planning throughout a person's lifetime. In addition, purchasing insurance against a variety of health and future care requirements is an obvious offset. And wise use of vehicles such as charitable lead and remainder trusts and other tax-effective arrangements can accomplish a happy medium of setting aside either current income or asset wealth, either for better living or charitable giving. The choice is the giver's.

Problem: Many people argue that a dollar given is a dollar (after tax savings) gone forever and worry that they will be unable to continue earning high rates of return on assets while alive. The natural tendency to preserve capital and not to dip into it has developed into an Eleventh Commandment of "Thou shalt not invade capital."

Solution: There are definitely times when such invasion is appropriate and even wise. Conservative withdrawals of capital can easily be tolerated by many; these delicate dips, so long as they are not repeated too often, are not the cause of problems. More important, the giving plans recommended here call only for short-term commitments and encourage constant reassessment of personal circumstances along the way. Finally, the trusts mentioned above offer equal or enhanced protection of income or asset wealth.

Problem: The opposite of extreme worry is the reluctance to relinquish capital because of high confidence that net worth can be multiplied significantly and that charities will benefit more if gifts are delayed until death.

Solution: While this can be true, the question is whether significant amounts shouldn't be given anyway by people who can afford it. It is shortsighted for those with reasonable life expectancy and sufficient assets to delay their giving when they could make positive, necessary contributions right now. Equally important, the history books are filled with examples of successful, wealthy investors who cannot repeat earlier grandiose accomplishments. In fact, there are many more such cases than of those who remain on a roll forever. (An excellent contemporary discussion of this can be found in John O'Neil's book *The Paradox of Success.*) For most people of means, an average rate of return is in store, and this is more than adequate protection to allow moderate, limited withdrawals.

Problem: Some people continue to claim there is an advantage to their families in waiting to die to make bequests to children or others. Since there are neither size limitations nor inheritance taxes on charitable contributions at death, procrastination is easily rationalized.

Solution: There are sound ways to start small and achieve important results for both family and philanthropic causes. For example, current laws allow individuals to give annual tax-free gifts of $10,000 to anyone of your choice. Many people also fail to utilize fully the federal government's allowed $600,000 personal lifetime gift to heirs. As to philanthropy, procrastinating about giving until death obviously means that needy causes can go wanting for too many years. Potential contributors also miss the joys of participating, the recognition, social acceptance, and heightened self-esteem that might accompany enlightened giving while alive.

Problem: The US tax system is seen by many as a deterrent. Once so favorably tilted that a giver could retain more after-tax dollars by giving (as opposed to selling a low-cost asset and keeping the proceeds), today's tax code does not provide this philanthropic encouragement. Currently there is a net cost to giving while you're alive versus waiting to give to charitable causes after death.

Solution: Deductions do remain. Gifts can also be efficiently made with securities that have low-cost bases that would be expensive to sell outright.

Problem: Relying on attorneys, accountants, financial planners, or other professionals to encourage greater giving is unrealistic. In fact, there is a reluctance on the part of such professionals to practice what they preach.

Solution: Sometimes these advisers have conflicts of interest in which a reduction of client wealth may decrease their own income. Often they defer because they see no urgency to recommend something they haven't researched adequately themselves or that they expect to be received negatively. One solution is to convince an adviser that your satisfaction will not be gauged solely by asset value. Judgment of their performance should parallel the definition of truly good friends: they should tell you what you need to know, not what they think you want or don't want to hear!

Problem: Section 1014 of the Internal Revenue Code of 1986 provides for a "stepped-up basis" for inherited assets, thus discouraging charitable gifts of holdings with very low costs. This includes real estate, where death of the owner provides heirs or beneficiaries a new, generally higher value of buildings and an opportunity to deduct more depreciation expense and create more tax-free cash flow.

Solution: This tax section definitely encourages people, particularly of older age, to hold on to their assets and not make lifetime gifts to charities or beneficiaries. Various charitable trusts can be convenient and tax-effective ways to utilize these low-cost assets. And there are ways for families to handle low-cost properties internally that make financial sense, too.

Problem: Just about the time that many people attain high wealth, they face the insecurities and conservatism that may accompany advancing age.

Solution: Under these circumstances, giving naturally suffers. But proper estate planning and use of certain tax-saving, insurance, or investment vehicles can overcome most worries. People of means should become well acquainted with all the various financial options and possibilities available to them. The more knowledge you have about your finances and the more confident you are that your strategies and planning are sensible, the less uncertainty and insecurity you will feel.

Category 2: Arguments That Require More General Advice, Including Pertinent Strategies for More Efficient or Wiser Giving

Problem: Frustration can result from not making a significant impact on causes through giving, as well as from not knowing how the money will be spent. People sometimes argue that the recipients will not handle the money wisely. Not knowing how to approach efficient, meaningful giving, they do nothing.

Solution: Countless charities have programs that specifically target the giver's goals; the organizations can and should provide answers to questions that will build confidence in their efficiency and effectiveness. The nonprofit National Charities Information Bureau (19 Union Square West, New York, New York 10003), Give But Give Wisely (4200 Wilson Boulevard, Arlington, Virginia 22203), and the National Philanthropic Advisory Service (PAS) of the Council of Better Business Bureaus (Dept. 023, Washington, DC, 20042-0023) can provide a contributor's checklist and guides to wise giving. *Forbes* and *Money* magazines are also now publishing annual rankings of numerous charities' percentages of income devoted to program services. Local charities are seldom covered, however, by any of these rating efforts. And financial information is not necessarily uniform among nonprofits, so interested donors should learn to do their own research (Chapter 21 provides good preparation for this). Excellent information also exists from community foundations and regional grantmaker associations who succeed in knowing which nonprofits are making a difference in cost-effective ways.

Category 3: Habits and Emotions That May Require Different "Skills" or Avenues of Improvement

Problem: Most philanthropy is erratic and uneven, not as methodical or thought out as it should be. With as many needy causes as there are, confusion is natural. Some of the wealthiest people are also the busiest, and they are probably badgered by solicitations that confuse and even anger them.

Solution: Giving by people in most income groups, including the very highest financial levels, is seldom well planned or systematic. But better giving habits can be developed. It is important to obtain objective advice and to seek out the right people and organizatons. References should be checked thoroughly. Also, be sure that advisers do not have conflicts of interest. Incidentally, one of the best advisers may be your spouse: turning over responsibility to your "better half" can accomplish wonders.

Problem: Some people equate success and failure with specific asset values. This can lead to an emotional attachment to certain levels of wealth.

Solution: "Keeping score" is a natural human tendency, and the accumulation of money is one precise means for measuring success. Unfortunately, once people have attained holdings of a given size, having anything less can make them feel less secure. Personal soul-searching may be needed to analyze why such insecurities exist. Certainly monetary gauges should not be the appropriate measure of human worth.

I once criticized a famous financial writer for glorifying someone because he had accumulated what, in certain New York City circles, was referred to as a "unit": $100 million. My point was that the highest accolades should have been reserved for the person who had "only" $50 million left but had given away $50 million. But apparently in a certain crowd, possessing a "unit" was the epitome of success — obviously a narrow measure.

As I mentioned earlier, our country's future will be enhanced as people shift their definitions of success away from strict monetary ones and toward community involvement, intellectual achievement, honesty, and similar criteria. If individuals are surrounded by people who place wealth above all else, new circles of friends and associates might be the solution.

Problem: As it is often the accepted gauge of success, money is also the "game of all games" — and one that never goes out of style. Winning and losing can become the sole focus, and some people may consider giving as simply surefire losing without a chance of winning.

Solution: There is nothing wrong with the "game" of money, so long as it doesn't obliterate the larger game of life. More will be said about this later, but think how we have slipped into bad word usage that may be influencing people in a negative way. I recently had a conversation with a good friend who lamented that he had come from what he labeled a "lower-class" family. He meant "lower income," but he said "lower class." I corrected him, insisting that people should reserve the "upper-class" distinction for those who exhibit excellence in community service, philanthropy, human service, and the like. Income and wealth alone should remain isolated — used for their monetary description alone.

Problem: Some people want privacy and do not want to attract attention to personal wealth by giving large sums.

Solution: Certainly privacy in today's world may be more important than in the past. The question is whether such fears are exaggerated and whether the end (privacy) justifies the means (not giving). If this is a rational concern for certain people of exceptional wealth, a logical solution is to give anonymously or through an intermediary: for example, through community foundations, organizations set up to serve as conduits for gifts to worthy nonprofits, through mutual funds set up for charitable gifts, or through your own separate vehicle for this purpose.

Problem: Too many people downplay their wealth to the point that they are unrealistic about what they can and cannot afford. And too many simply misuse the word "afford" altogether.

Solution: With my breakthroughs, affordability can (and should) be more scientifically measured, so this may be less of a problem than people think. Furthermore, the expression "can't afford" is used inconsistently and has become a convenient rationale and knee-jerk excuse. For example, parents often use the phrase with their children, substituting "can't afford" for the real reason, which may be that they simply do not want to spend the money for fear it will spoil the children. Or, they use the term because they can't bear to say no.

As you can see, some of the preceding arguments against philanthropy are rational, others are exaggerated, and still others are just plain manufactured. But most of the arguments against enhanced giving are easily addressed — and in ways that are relatively painless. Most important, the positives to be derived from philanthropy are not fully understood. While improving our society and curing its ills are obvious attractions, the personal and familial advantages giving affords are far more constructive than most people realize. Experimenting with the Reaching Out concept can introduce greater happiness to millions of Americans and their families.

Chapter 12

Protecting Yourself Against the Worst

WHAT is financially sensible and what is reckless in increasing your charitable giving or in improving your standard of living?

Living standards and giving (particularly with its tax deductibility) can often be substantially enhanced without frittering away assets, without falling into an investment hole, without neglecting financial obligations or inheritances, and without doing anything that will create traumas or endanger financial security and peace of mind.

Declining asset levels can occur, however, and in many ways. For our purposes, it is most important to understand that, barring unforeseen catastrophes, investing can be diversified in a way that should preclude the most drastic, devastating results.

Naturally, there is a price to pay for this protection. Diversification into a variety of investment instruments, which is the most logical approach to such safety, eliminates the potential for the total "home run," but it can provide steady, reasonably good results and eliminate the investing "strikeout." Diversification also minimizes certain excuses for not giving. This is not to say that giving ought to be the sole reason for diversification: there is good reason for people fortunate enough to have attained high asset and income levels to protect what they have amassed and to guarantee that they will never be deprived of whatever standard of living they choose to retain.

But what if, even with diversification, a person's investments

Table 6: Impact of Spending Versus Not Spending Followed by a
90 Percent Loss of Capital

	1	2
	Spending 10% of Capital Before Loss	*Not Spending Before Loss*
Original capital	$1,000,000	$1,000,000
Less extra spending	(100,000)	0
Capital before investment loss	900,000	1,000,000
Less 90% loss	(810,000)	(900,000)
REMAINING NET WORTH	$ 90,000	$ 100,000

are slated for disaster? Wouldn't reducing capital have been a bad choice? To answer, let's hypothesize that a worldwide financial catastrophe strikes and there are no investment places to hide. Or perhaps a personal catastrophe overwhelms someone and his or her net worth is decimated after having invaded capital for either living or giving purposes during better times.

As horrible as this all sounds, the truth is that delicate dipping into capital will not have been the cause of the problem. To illustrate, let's assume a near-worst-case scenario: a 90 percent loss of a $1 million corpus. Table 6 shows how the corpus would be affected. Column 1 assumes a spending of 10 percent of the capital before the loss; column 2 posits the loss without such spending.

The difference? All of $10,000, or 1 percent of the original capital! So it's clear that the prior drawdown of capital is not the culprit. Actually it's even less than 1 percent if the $100,000 has been a charitable contribution. Assuming the giver's marginal tax rate is 40 percent, the $100,000 donation became a net cost of $60,000, leaving $940,000. A 90 percent decline reduces this figure to $94,000 (not $90,000 as shown in Table 6). So the shortfall versus no giving is $6,000, or six-tenths of 1 percent of the original $1 million. It certainly has not been the straw that broke the camel's back or the cause for extra remorse. In fact, someone in this situation might even wish that he or she had tapped more of the principal before the catastrophe occurred.

Chart G shows how little the remaining net worth has been

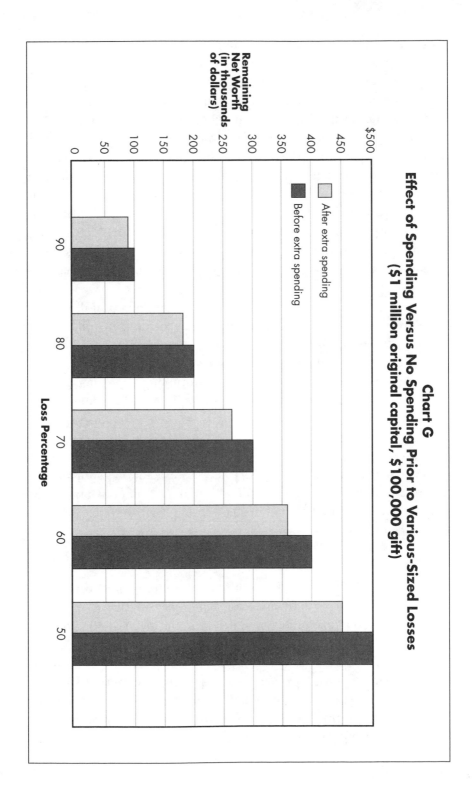

Chart G
Effect of Spending Versus No Spending Prior to Various-Sized Losses
($1 million original capital, $100,000 gift)

affected by a 10 percent withdrawal preceding the hypothesized loss. Ironically, the greater the loss ultimately suffered, the smaller the withdrawal's impact on the remaining net worth.

This is not to belittle the shrinkage of capital — perhaps the paramount investment consideration. Nor is this reasoning intended to overlook the natural human remorse that would erase the objectivity of an analysis such as the above. There are, however, ways to set up "rainy day" reserves to avoid such experiences whether or not you have dipped into capital.

More on Dipping into Capital

One of the largest roadblocks to giving or to spending on better living is the tendency of many people to deem invading capital as sacrilegious. A story from Amy Domini's fine book *Challenges of Wealth* makes the point.

> A Boston Brahmin was suddenly accosted by a "lady of the evening." Horrified, he turned toward her with "a look that had kept ten generations of inferiors in their places," when with even greater horror he saw the woman's face. "Cousin Louisa," he exclaimed, "what are you doing?" Looking him straight in the eye, she declared, "Elliott, it was either this or dip into capital!"

People consumed with Cousin Louisa's fears have overgeneralized as often as they have overreacted. They are frequently reluctant to consider the growth of their capital, as they often ignore the surplus income that is slated to add to their net worth. So it is no wonder that they are frightened by the thought of invading principal and that they allow this fear to become the excuse for inconsistent financial practices. No doubt philanthropy is a major victim of such thinking. Legitimacy of the argument against invading capital depends on the extent to which such dipping is practiced. Small dips should hardly be considered dangerous for people of reasonable means, just as larger, proportionate slices from massive holdings can be easily tolerated. Why shouldn't Cousin Louisa dip lightly into her capital in order to live well? And

why shouldn't a person with $100 million have a plan to give away
$50 million over time?

There are other reasons not to be so narrowly focused or skit-
tish about tapping capital. For example, there are obviously many
exceptions to the general rule that income and assets go together.
Some very wealthy people have relatively low income. Consider
certain land-rich or asset-rich people who generate low income.
Or owners of common stocks that pay meager or no cash dividends, like Bill Gates, founder and multibillionaire shareholder of
Microsoft, or Berkshire-Hathaway's amazing investor and chairman, Warren Buffett. Or thousands of others, whose combined
wealth might total in the hundreds of billions. People in these positions certainly shouldn't ignore sizable giving simply because
their income pales in relation to their net worth. Similar imbal-
ances can also exist for those with business accounting write-offs
that overwhelm reported income and actually disguise wealth of
any definition.

Too often, low-givers or nongivers rationalize that the absence
of substantial amounts of either income or assets constitutes good
reason not to give to charities or live more comfortably. For example, a doctor complained to me that he couldn't afford to donate to
a worthy cause because his very ample income wasn't combined
with substantial assets. Yet only a day later, I failed to convince an
immensely wealthy property owner that he should give to that
same cause because, as he responded with a straight face, "I don't
have the income" (it was sheltered by tax write-offs and the use of
overseas tax havens).

What was the difference between this property owner's position and the billionaire examples? Should he have considered his
low income or even the absence of income a reason not to live
comfortably or give to charity? Why should he consider himself
the equivalent of a poor person who has little or no responsibility
to help others? My point is that low-income/high-wealth people
generally can expand their gifting horizons, too; they have the
same responsibility as others with means and can usually find a
way to remedy the imbalance of their situation. Where there's a
will there's generally a way to use low-income assets beneficially.

Some people might even consider selling off portions of their considerable nonearning assets, slowly and reasonably, in order to raise their living standards, to provide for their families, or — without depriving themselves — to give to a cause they support. Trading negative-cash-flow (due to property taxes) raw land in exchange for income property is one solution. At death, inheritance taxes will need to be paid, and some of the assets will probably need to be sold anyway by heirs to meet these obligations. Or consider gifting or selling a property where living privileges are retained by you and your spouse through your lifetimes. Why not consider ways to access asset values now, before they are sacrificed in other ways?

High-income/low-asset people like the doctor also have room to expand: here the potential should relate to the size and stability of their earnings. In some cases, the source can be insured in some way; if, for example, bequests are the roadblock, low-cost term life insurance might provide an offset. In most cases, the probabilities for continuance of income are favorable.

Naturally, it is crucial to assess how one's capital and income might fare in the future, both on an absolute and a relative basis. How much spending, future investing, and giving can be accommodated? How large a decline in purchasing power (eroded by inflation or by unsuccessful investments) can be tolerated? This can be determined by using the "lifelong financial statement" approach of Breakthrough 4. Exceptions exist here, too, such as a wealthy ninety-year-old who should no longer worry much about outliving sizable assets, or the person whose fortune is so great that even a drastic decline will still leave a high-enough level of assets to provide a lifetime of comfortable living.

Remember, asset values are naturally enhanced or depleted in relation to whether income is adequate or inadequate for taxes, spending, giving, and so on. What's adequate or inadequate defies a generalization that will cover everyone. But just as Breakthrough 1 showed a reasonable zone for normal spending, there is a level that will allow for taxes, enough increment to capital to keep up with inflation, and, also, more generous contributions, more comfortable living, or both. Before expanding on the former, let's discuss the logic of tapping reasonable amounts of capital solely for enhanced living.

Chapter 13

Breaking the Habit of Self-Deprivation

I HAVE talked less about increasing expenditures to enhance living standards than to make charitable donations, which at least possess the advantage of tax savings. But a similar philosophy pertains to daily living, even though additional spending has no such advantage.

Needless to say, if a person with minor assets starts depleting capital, the risk is that a nest egg will never be built. Sadly, many people have little choice and not only draw down consistently from reserves but actually incur debt — to the point that they have negative net worth. Obviously, this is not recommended.

This book, however, is aimed mainly at people who directly or indirectly have assets to back up earning power, yet who might fall into the "I can't afford" syndrome despite contrary factual evidence. While there will always be exceptions, many people seem absolutely intent on punishing themselves unnecessarily.

The following story is bizarre but true. The uncle of a good friend of mine was seventyish and extremely affluent. Yet he invariably took overnight airline trips on which, seated in the back of the plane, he was squeezed between other passengers, was unable to sleep, and couldn't even read leisurely. One day my friend decided to convince his uncle to travel first-class, to avoid the wear and tear, enjoy the service, and, perhaps, draw pleasure from the whole experience.

Uncle Alfred needed some convincing. "At what point does one decide he can afford to fly first-class?" he asked.

His nephew's response was classic. "I may not know all the criteria, but I'm damned sure that anyone who can afford to buy a brand-new 747 for cash — which you could do if you chose — definitely qualifies!"

It would be difficult to match my friend's convincing argument, but I would hope that the breakthrough spreadsheets might also have tilted Uncle Alfred's conservatism more toward practicality. Although he respects frugality, the nephew also chided Uncle Alfred: "You not only can afford to fly first-class, but you should also realize that one day all your grandchildren will probably be flying first-class and possibly joking about why you hadn't done so, too!"

Uncle Alfred doesn't travel often anymore, but when he does, he no longer endures the discomforts of coach seats, and his first few days after reaching his destination are far more enjoyable for being well rested.

The Uncle Alfred tale is obviously exceptional. Similar stories at lower wealth levels and lesser (but more meaningful) sacrifices exist. I have seen people who can afford to buy dozens of garages search endlessly for free parking. I've heard of people who could buy whole grocery chains literally starving themselves. And, perhaps more to the point, I've seen people deprive themselves of wonderful opportunities for personal, philanthropic, and humanitarian satisfaction, mainly because of the fear of dipping ever so slightly into income, much less capital.

Naturally, it is more prudent not to invade principal. But the basic philosophical questions remain: Just what is money's purpose? How important is it to leave the maximum to heirs? Are huge inheritances even wise? Does it make sense to cling to large amounts of capital and consider it a defeat to allow the sums to fall below some magical, more-than-adequate value? These are questions people should ask themselves. And they should add another: When should capital be used? Yes, not if, but when.

The best reasons to consider occasional and limited capital withdrawals are precisely because they are occasional and limited.

Income and capital should be considered as a team. And intelligent use of net worth is not, therefore, a cardinal sin.

Thus, it is generally not a question of "To dip, or not to dip." It often boils down to how much to tap, and how often. If we're discussing, say, 2 percent of corpus over and above income, with withdrawals held to predetermined, limited periods, is financial security being endangered? Simple mathematics say no — assuming, of course, that one's net worth has positive earnings, that liquidity of capital exists, that health and housing costs are covered, that inflation isn't obliterating purchasing power, and that withdrawals are reassessed yearly.

A Classic Case of Delicate Dipping for Personal Necessities

Take the case of Widow Jones. She has been left a $500,000 corpus of earning assets that provide a 6 percent annual income of $30,000. Looking at income alone, particularly income after taxes, which have reduced the $30,000 to, say, between $22,000 and $23,000, Mrs. Jones has good reason to worry about covering her living expenses and buying occasional gifts for her grandchildren, much less affording an annual vacation for herself.

But should she feel strapped and traumatized about her future? Perhaps not. Although her picture cannot be converted to one of total affluence, a conservative withdrawal plan toward her more comfortable living can be justified. Assuming she has the basics of health insurance and housing covered, Mrs. Jones might safely withdraw $10,000, or 2 percent, on a five-year basis from her $500,000 net worth. If such withdrawal comes from cash or assets without low cost basis, little or no income tax will result; hence, her after-tax spending potential rises from $22,000–$23,000 to $32,000–$33,000 — a huge difference. This $10,000 withdrawal seems prudent only if you assume that perhaps $200,000–$250,000 is invested in an asset like common stocks, whose value can be expected to appreciate over time. If, for example, Mrs. Jones owns stock that might grow in value on average 6 to 8 percent, or $12,000 to $20,000 per year, some cushion exists. But capital appreciation is not guaranteed — it is bound to be volatile and unpredictable. So caution is always the byword, and capital withdrawals should be very occasional, very small, or both unless the combination of income and assets owned is significant in relation to withdrawal needs.

Do not assume, however, that Widow Jones is elderly and that the principal of tapping capital is feasible only for people of advanced age. A young couple in their thirties, possibly the recipients of an inheritance, might employ the same prudent technique. The purpose might differ: perhaps the delicate dipping might support home mortgage payments, or allow for improved education for their children — but the logic of the affordability criteria would be similar.

Of course, it's one thing if Widow Jones or the young couple want to take out $25,000 on a regular basis to improve their standard of living. It's also different if they use the money for great extravagances. But an occasional $10,000 to live more comfortably should not cause traumas — again, providing that net worth is unburdened by debts, is adequately hedged against dramatic declines, and is growing in line with purchasing needs and desires. Again, withdrawals must be reassessed for prudence yearly.

Anyone contemplating major increased expenditures or delicate dips into capital should consider

- age, tempered by the ability to replace depleted assets (withdrawals by a seventy-year-old may be more appropriate than for a thirty-year-old because of expected life span, but the latter probably has superior earning potential);
- health and adequacy of health insurance protection;
- bequest desires;
- housing stability and costs (whether the residence is fully paid for or, in the case of a renter, there is some protection against excessive rental increases);
- the definition of necessities (it will no doubt include education for children, but it may also include their housing, braces for grandchildren, and so on);
- liquidity of assets owned; and
- quality and stability of the earning assets.

Given the caveats already expressed, it should be reassuring to know that the tables on giving, and the estimating of net worth amounts, certainly apply to standards of living, too. Pardon the repetition, but remember that invasion of corpus should not be practiced indiscriminately. It must be carefully analyzed and not considered without the kind of affordability filters presented here. Approached this way, it should be given equal consideration along with other financial decisions, and it is often a viable option.

Chapter 14

Affording to Invest More in Yourself or Your Community

WHILE one would hope that people who break from unnecessary deprivation might choose philanthropy for at least a portion of their enhanced living, let's concentrate now solely on enhanced giving by those who are already spending adequately and can well afford to do more. Let me emphasize, though, that all recommendations here must be considered as generalizations to be altered based on individual circumstances, tax regulations, and stability of income and assets; and that competent tax counsel is a must for anyone contemplating greatly enhanced giving.

Inputs have already shown that the 1991 high-end IRS group has substantial surplus wealth. While it is impossible to assume precisely how much surplus exists, certainly the old habit of concentrating solely on income is shortsighted. Consider how imprudent it is to ignore the capital appreciation potentials of an owner's investments.

A pivotal question is whether somebody with a conservatively stated EA of $16 million should risk any reduction in inflation-adjusted assets. Suggested donation levels do not always imply reductions. Still, if people with this wealth cannot give an amount that portends a moderate decrease in their healthy EA on an inflation-adjusted basis, how can we expect those of lesser means to share much, if anything at all?

An earlier discussion suggested that the top AGI/EA group average could apparently afford to hike their 1991 donation level of $87,000 to $900,000 (approximately $540,000 after tax deductions) in one year and still retain a "real" amount equal to 3.8 percent *more* than their initial $16 million. Certainly the donation is not of staggering proportion on this basis! Certainly it is not significant enough to warrant fears about future financial security, especially if the donor follows the practical, prudent advice to make regular reassessments of both the critical elements, income *and* earning assets.

Another variable to consider when determining net worth is *non*earning assets — possessions such as homes, antiques, collections, raw land, and so forth. Interpretation of two IRS estate surveys suggests that it makes sense to add at least $3 million in nonearning wealth to the highest-average-taxpayer's $16 million EA, thereby bringing total wealth to over $19 million. Suffice it to say that these calculations are conservative, since the government's own estate-based *total* asset figure for a comparable earning level suggests much higher total asset estimates.

Keep in mind that the example above has concentrated on a single dollar amount. Recommendations for other levels, below and above this average, will be different. Suggested giving levels in both absolute and percentage terms will obviously vary, dependent on the amount and the makeup of the AGI and EA levels.

Finally, despite all the calculations, do not assume that any of the figures used in our examples are meant to be exact. Individuals in identical income and wealth categories can differ dramatically in a broad array of circumstances. Thus, there is no single number that applies to all — but those in a given category can at least know what might be affordable. And most can now justify, certainly in financial terms, and perhaps in a philosophical way, too, far more philanthropic giving than the records show they have allowed themselves.

The Impact of the First Illustration of Enlightened Giving

Given the total universe of "Over $1 million AGI" taxpayers, the combination of many additional $813,000 gifts to worthy charities holds unbelievable potential. Converting the $87,000 donation to $900,000 amounts to a 903 percent (10.3 times) improvement. In 1991, this increment would have raised the IRS total donations from $4.5 billion to a staggering $46.3 billion. Even with participation in enhanced giving limited to this one high-income group, the possibilities for very large net gains to society are enormous. What remains, then, is to prove without a doubt that there are no other significant risks associated with expanded giving and that proposed levels for lower-income groups are equally affordable and safe.

A Quick Review of Affordability and Assumptions

Before going further, let's briefly review the concept of surplus money and see how prudently and conservatively it was constructed. After all, no one should be expected to convert from "can't afford" to "can't afford not to" without airtight financial proof.

First, everyone has been forewarned that each situation must be considered separately. Each person's income and assets must be assured, housing and living expenses given priority, and health insurance put in place before any additional expenditure is considered.

Second, future net worth possibilities are calculated based on the sharply higher income tax rates existent in 1994, and little factoring has been made for individuals' abilities to lower their average tax rates significantly below the marginal rates.

Third, the living expenses deducted from spendable income are liberal.

Fourth, investment return assumptions have been lowered from the 1991 data conclusions. Interest rates are assumed to be over 100 basis points (1 percent) below the 1991 realities.

Moreover, my recommendations include a margin for error by allowing large additions to net worth for all but the extremely wealthy (of course, the others cannot expect much growth unless they have sufficient discretionary income to begin with). The very wealthy are protected too: their EAs either grow moderately or (at the highest levels) remain static on an inflation-adjusted basis. Even a dipping by the latter into at least 1 to 3 percent of net worth would not be a dangerous, imprudent approach to consider, especially for a period of five years and factoring in tax savings.

As mentioned, using IRS-reported income as a base for net worth calculations further cushions my definition of affordability, since even the IRS acknowledges that income reported to the government is markedly below real levels. In addition, my projections for common stocks, which constitute 45 percent of the top-bracket net worth estimates, could have been increased substantially to allow for the significant wealth now concentrated in lower-dividend-paying companies such as Microsoft, Wal-Mart, Berkshire-Hathaway, and numerous others.

In short, I do not take capital withdrawals lightly, and I have tilted assumptions to the conservative side. The lower the EA, therefore, the less that has been recommended for giving, since it is obvious that more capital is needed to concentrate on building assets and net worth. For those with more than a few million in earning assets, the donation weightings are progressively increased as net worth grows. In short, the goal is to ensure rapid buildup of principal for lower asset groups, more moderate increases for medium-to-higher wealth groups, and no buildup or moderate declines for the very wealthy.

Chapter 15

Maximizing the Time Value of Money

ALBERT EINSTEIN once remarked facetiously that the most amazing discovery of his life was how interest on money compounds. His comment was not without merit, for Einstein understood how small changes in monetary costs or returns can balloon into massive amounts over time. Conversely, we have to be careful that suggestions for relatively minor financial commitments — short or long term — do not endanger net worth.

Up to now I've focused on the short-term effects of varying drawdowns on income or capital. As important as these are, it is imperative to consider their cumulative effects.

Consider these fundamental questions:

- How do repeated withdrawals of higher portions of income and moderate EA usage affect net worth over many years?
- Will such withdrawals still allow for financial security or will they lead to ruin? Will they yield peace of mind or excessive worry?
- How much more vulnerable to investment setbacks are portfolios geared toward recurring, more generous giving or enhanced living?
- Can the reduction of net worth from such withdrawals still allow for inheritance needs?
- How will increased giving affect all of the above?

Totally precise answers to these questions are impossible. The behavior of economies and investment markets and their effects on the value of an infinite number and variety of assets and income sources are simply too complex and uncertain to permit exact predictions. However, realistic numbers that permit reasoned analyses and well-documented financial conclusions can be produced.

Prior chapters have concentrated heavily on how much giving might be tolerated by a person in 1991's highest income bracket — a $1.825 million earner with $16 million in earning assets. Although results were presented for one set of investment assumptions, different experiences would have resulted from other projections. These might include (1) negative investment returns leading to a possibly sizable reduction in an earning-asset value below $16 million; (2) positive returns producing more than $16 million in EAs but not matching inflation; (3) increments that barely cover inflation or slightly exceed it; and (4) bonanza returns that produce sharply higher earning assets and very positive real returns.

We have seen how, even under horrible conditions, the "extra" $813,000/total $900,000 giving (around $540,000 after taxes) would not have been the crucial consideration. If the $16 million with*out* extra giving dropped a horrid 90 percent, the 10 percent remainder would total but $1.6 million; whereas if the base had become $15.46 million due to the $540,000 after-tax contributions that preceded the investment shrinkage, the 10 percent left would be $1.546 million, or $54,000 less.

Since 90 percent, or even 50 percent, reductions in value are certainly the exception and not the rule, let's assess the risks from this additional $813,000 contribution in other ways. First, the $813,000 amounts to $488,000 after the $325,000 tax deduction. Second, our Table 5 Worksheet (pages 74–75) that included 1991's $87,000 donation showed a $571,000 surplus of income after all expenses and taxes—a cushion of $83,000 before the initial principal is impaired. Third, dividing the $488,000 after-tax cost into two equal JASS portions of $244,000 amounts to 13.3 percent of AGI and 1.5 percent of EA—not outsized proportions given the high income and asset wealth involved.

Still, we have to probe further to determine whether additional withdrawals or poor investment results could lead to diminishing net worth, jeopardizing financial security or obligations. As mentioned, the difference of but a few percentage points in compounding annual returns can amount to dramatic amounts of money over many years. Thus, it is crucial to prove without a doubt that additional giving (or living expenses) in the proportions suggested is safe.

Before comparing nongiving, normal giving, and more elevated giving (and before considering further the effects of simply withdrawing capital), it is important to understand the "time value of money" concepts that sophisticated investors live by.

A Primer on the Time Value of Money and on Present Values

The "time value of money" suggests that unless there is deflation, a dollar given to you a year from now provides less purchasing power than the same amount given today. And one dollar received five years from now will be worth even less. Under normal conditions, you will be able to buy less with that future payment than you could if you had access to it now. So dollars in the mattress are a bad idea. Even if you have no spending plans, you should start earning something in today's dollars — even money in the safest of investments may soon be worth more.

Whether the intention is buying or earning, therefore, people should think about the "time value of money" especially in terms of "present value." A lottery winner is a good example. Is a person who wins $50,000 a year for twenty years actually a millionaire? No. Using an earning-assumption (usually called "discount") rate of 5 percent, the $1 million in payments over twenty years is really worth the equivalent of only $623,111 today. This $623,111 is called the "present value" amount that, in this case, earns at an annual 5 percent rate and guarantees $50,000 income per year for twenty years.

Why must present values of money be understood? Because conclusions about nongiving, moderate giving, and generous giving must reflect the respective time values of the three different giving approaches. Similarly, you should spend capital only with the knowledge that the net worth is safe on an inflation-adjusted basis. Seeing all future figures in present-value terms allows for accurate comparisons and inflation adjustments.

Using the concepts of time value and present value, let's return to those $1.825 million annual earners and ask: How much can they afford to give over a longer period?

Breakthrough 4's spreadsheets show income figures for the first year that parallel actual 1991 IRS data. Then, logical assumptions about earned income, capital appreciation, living expenses, taxes, and contributions are made for subsequent years, to arrive at an estimated net worth at the end of each year. The mix of investments and income sources also closely mirrors IRS data in all years. Hence, there is a diversification of income and assets, with salaries and business-type income blended with holdings of bonds, common stocks, and real property. This blend produces an average of what exists for older or very conservative investors along with younger or more aggressive ones. The diversification includes enough assets and resources to provide reasonable, but obviously not guaranteed, protection from the separate extreme risks of either high deflation or high inflation.

Three Comparisons

My goal is to compare the estimated growth of three identical beginning financial positions in which income from bonds has been lowered and marginal tax rates raised to reflect conditions prevailing in early 1994, but with three different charitable giving levels: (1) a nongiving portfolio, versus (2) an identical one that incorporates giving typical of 1991 data ($87,000), versus (3) the suggested new contribution level. This third level uses assigned ratios to income and earning assets that produce a donation level of $900,000 in the first year and then applies the same ratios to subsequent income and EA experience over a five-year period. Here are the after-debt, rounded-figure characteristics of this high-end portfolio:

Total net worth value	$19,000,000
Earning assets that have capitalized value (because they generate income)	16,000,000
Nonearning assets	3,000,000

First year's total charitable contribution	900,000
Blended interest rate yield from taxable and tax-exempt bonds	5.5%
Dividend yield on common stocks	2.5%
Earning assets breakdown	
Bonds	33%
Stocks	45%
Real estate	5%
Other EA	17%
Annual price appreciation from bonds	0
Annual price appreciation from stocks	7%
Annual price appreciation from real estate and other EA	3%
Salaries and wages	$715,000[a]
First year's living expenses	$590,000[a]
Ordinary-income tax rate	39.6%[b,c]
Capital-gains tax rate	28%[c]
Inflation rate	3%
Periods under consideration	1–30 years

[a] After the first year, the assumption is for growth at an inflation rate of 3% per year.

[b] Estimated federal tax rate. No assumption made for state income taxes, which can range from zero to double digit levels, but no assumptions either for significant deductions other than for charitable donations.

[c] With ownership of tax-exempt bonds and other deductions, the average tax rate on AGI normally runs well below the highest marginal rate. The 1991 average for this group was 26% excluding state taxes (29% including state levies).

In line with the suggestion to consider a limited initial period of higher donations, the model assumes that giving reverts to 1991's "percentage to charities" levels after the fifth year.

Obviously, any portfolios that include giving are bound to be smaller than those that don't. Table 7 describes this high-income-bracket taxpayer under the three levels of giving, projected over five- and ten-year spans.

Table 7 Discussed

Line b in Table 7 ("Earning assets — present value") shows the all-important inflation-adjusted values generated for all three giving levels over the two projected periods. Remember that earning

Table 7: Estimated Giving Effects for 1991's IRS Top Earning Group
($16 million EA, $1.825 million AGI excluding capital gains)
(dollar figures in millions)

	1	2	3	4	5	6
	No Giving		*1991's Average Giving*		*Elevated Giving*	
	After Year		*After Year*		*After Year*	
	5	10	5	10	5	10
a Earning assets — nominal	$22.62	$31.80	$22.28	$30.89	$19.32	$26.96
b Earning assets — present value	$19.51	$23.66	$19.22	$22.98	$16.67	$20.06
c After-tax rate of return on present value EA	4.0%	4.0%	3.7%	3.7%	0.8%	2.3%
d Total contributions — present value	0	0	$0.45	$0.98	$4.43	$4.89
e Total contributions — after tax, present value	0	0	$0.27	$0.59	$2.68	$2.96

assets only have been accounted for; homes, possessions, and similar nonearning assets (estimated to be at minimum $3 million) have been excluded and provide another fudge factor in the judgment of affordability.

This is a five-year plan, so let's first look at comparative earning-asset values of the three levels of giving after those five years. Looking again at line b and rounding, we note that columns 1, 3, and 5 show the following

Present-value net worths:

Nongivers	$19.5 million
Average 1991 givers	$19.2 million
Higher givers	$16.7 million

The $16.7 million is 13 to 14 percent less than the respective $19.2 and $19.5 million outcomes from the other giving categories. But the higher giving still produces an inflation-adjusted EA that is 4.2 percent above the initial $16.0 million corpus. Despite elevating the donation from $87,000 to $900,000, the giver is in an improved relative economic condition as at the start. Columns 2, 4, and 6 of line b show the plausible wealth levels after a ten-year span. Here are those present-value net worths after rounding:

Nongivers	$23.7 million
Average 1991 givers	$23.0 million
Higher givers	$20.1 million

All three groups are now substantially above the starting level of $16 million. This shows that ample inflation protection and other safeguards have existed. The difference between nongivers and average givers is $0.7 million, and the difference between average and higher givers is $2.9 million. Interesting to note in line e of Table 7 are the zeros of the nongivers' contributions to charities compared to the after-tax present-value donations of $0.27 million and $0.59 million (in columns 3 and 4) for the 1991 average givers and the $2.68 million and $2.96 million (in columns 5 and 6) for the elevated-giving-level group over the first five and ten years.

In short, the financial "sacrifices" of increased giving will hardly have been devastating, while the relative contributions to the community will have been very important. Said another way, higher givers can do a lot, feel better about themselves, and not endanger their financial security. As a matter of fact, they have retained their inflation-adjusted wealth during their five years of higher giving and exceeded it thereafter. A win-win-win for all.

Chapter 16

Overcoming the Uncertainties of Net Worth and Income

IN addition to poor health and similar catastrophes, there are five major risks to an individual's financial security, risks that may have an effect on the advisability of dipping into discretionary income or into capital.

The first risk is the stability of personal earning power — that is, how one's job, profession, or business income will fare in the future. Needless to say, this can only be assessed by each individual. For these purposes, I have assumed that the initial average earning figure (from salaries and personal businesses) grows in line with an assumed inflation rate of approximately 3 percent. Thus, barring catastrophe and assuming a steady earning or inflation rate, insecurities concerning future personal earning power should not overwhelm the ideas of spending or giving more.

The second major risk is what happens to investments that constitute the bulk of net worth and that normally provide significant income, too. Results will range from very successful to disastrous, but one practical approach is to project smoothed average returns over the years. As indicated, longer holding periods (ten years or more) for common stocks and bonds have produced consistently positive, though varying, returns to their owners — with significantly higher returns and greater volatility for equities than for fixed-income investments.

Past performance of real estate is not easily or readily measurable. Real-property indexes equivalent to the S&P or the Dow Jones Industrial Average are not available for long periods, nor are there enough real estate mutual funds that provide comparable records. Further complications exist because of the heavier borrowing normally involved and the many years of tax advantages associated with real property. Despite the very poor results experienced in real estate since the mid- to late 1980s, longer spans have probably experienced patterns similar to stocks.

Comfortable living levels vary according to personal tastes, as do definitions of surplus money. I have factored suggested contribution and eventual EA goals for all of the above. Since recommended after-tax withdrawals detract only moderately from potential net worth additions, and since the recommended increased giving plan has been limited to a five-year trial period, there appears to be ample safety.

Any investor who is heavily leveraged with debt or is involved in highly speculative investments may go from feast to famine; but the vast majority — people who manage their investments in a reasonably conservative way — should expect their fortunes to fluctuate less and to prosper reasonably well over time.

The third risk is the volatility of values (and possibly income) that will occur, particularly over shorter spans — normally over one-, two-, or three-year periods. Again, the proposed increments in withdrawal amounts will not create or exacerbate this volatility. Increased giving at the suggested levels is *not* the culprit and it neither spells disaster nor even contributes significantly to it. Diversification of assets is a hedge against such volatility, as well as a generally sound investment practice — and a spread of investments is exactly what has been assumed in the models presented.

The fourth risk is retention of purchasing power, which means ensuring that income and net worth keep up with inflation. While usually more subtle, the quantitative models herein support the thesis that more giving is both affordable and safe for many, even after accounting for inflation — assuming, of course, that it does not run rampant for extended periods and, again, that overall investment conditions are not disastrous.

The fifth risk is less tangible, but important. It is the emotional factors — the traumas — that even temporary setbacks from the first four risks might create. We cannot expect an individual whose earning power or net worth has depreciated much in either nominal or real terms to feel very relaxed or particularly generous during such times.

No one can eliminate the nervousness and uncertainties that accompany such an experience. Diversification of assets or earning power can mitigate losses, which in turn can reduce traumas, but owning various types of assets is no ironclad guarantee against losses, even significant downturns, either. Knowing that time should ultimately work to the investor's favor can help. Still, there are no guarantees, other than to make sure that there is enough cushion to withstand both temporary and longer-lasting disappointments — a cushion I consider essential when recommending small relative invasions of income or capital.

Shelter for a Rainy Day

There are, in fact, ways to establish "cushions" against feared or unforeseen negative experiences — cushions that need not seriously affect overall investment results.

One simple mechanism is to set up a "rainy-day fund" that (1) is invested in the safest, least volatile, shorter term Treasury securities and (2) is the equivalent of, say, five or even more years of income as an "insurance" reserve and (3) is earmarked to be used only in the event of emergency.

Such reserve funds often have an unanticipated fringe benefit. They can become much more than hedges or defensive pots of money if, for example, they bolster and encourage very positive, even aggressive, investing postures with the remaining, usable funds. One valued client of my firm did exactly this back in the mid-1970s. Faced with investing sizable funds after selling a family business, he convinced his relatives that an impenetrable, zero-risk fund that constituted just 15 to 20 percent of their assets was sufficient protection to allow them to keep 80 or 85 percent in higher-reward equities.

History had shown equities to be superior to fixed-income instruments over many decades, provided that an investor had the patience to withstand the inevitable near-term volatility of these assets. The family was determined to consider the 80 to 85 percent investment in common stocks just as it had viewed the business before selling it — not worrying about low valuations potential buyers might have placed on the enterprise from time to time, but focusing on its longer-range prospects. This strategy, which was psychologically reinforced by the existence of the reserve fund, produced many millions of dollars of additional net worth to them over the ensuing years.

Unfortunately, owners of real estate cannot always avail themselves of the liquidity to set up reserve funds. Tempering mortgage debts is one solution, however, as is refinancing (and setting aside these funds for reserves) when property values appear high or when mortgage rates are low. Owners of common stock can use other techniques, such as occasionally writing options directly against specific holdings, or using comparable riskless hedges against significant declines in market value.

So, cushioning can be both defensive and offensive, and it certainly can soften or eliminate fears that might otherwise interfere with sophisticated investing. Intelligent sheltering can actually improve everyday living, provide greater peace of mind, and perhaps even lead to greater charitable giving. In fact, there is no reason why individuals who rank giving as important shouldn't establish financial shelters for that purpose, too. As investment consultant Jan Greer said to me one day, "Having money earmarked for pursuits like giving is probably the best way to ensure its best use. It's when the days are darkest that people doubt their convictions most — and neglecting something as important as philanthropy when it is most needed is indeed a sad affair."

Chapter 17

How Lower-Income Groups Fit In

ALTHOUGH there will always be exceptions, lower-income earners generally possess sharply lower net worth, and they face higher relative spending needs, especially for essentials. They are also burdened with more pressing inheritance needs; that is, they face greater difficulty in providing comfortable living standards for their survivors.

The only relative advantage to lower income is in the area of taxation: rates on ordinary income can be a small fraction of what the highest earners pay. Inheritance taxes graduate the same way. The trade-offs, of course, distinctly favor higher-income earners. This is why living and giving provisions should be graduated downward as total incomes decrease — which is what this book's models recommend.

But lower-income groups can still maneuver within their own financial constraints to improve their standards of living or even to contribute more to society. They can make modest but meaningful financial contributions as income permits, in addition to volunteering to help particularly worthy causes in their local communities.

Table 2 on page 51 shows the estimated spending needs for seven income brackets, ranging from more than $1 million in annual income down to a $25,000–$50,000 range. I have already discussed the top income bracket and its earners' ability to save —

or spend — disproportionately more than those in the lower brackets. The spending needs of others — that is, with income ranging from $35,500 to $1 million annually — still project discretionary saving or additional spending potential of anywhere from approximately 4 percent to 36 percent of their income. My discussion here will not concentrate on income groups below $75,000, whose excess income after expenses is estimated to be 13 percent or less. And although the term "lower income" may be used in referring to them, the $75,000-and-above earners have sufficient income and earning assets to allow them room to consider broadened allocations to their, or society's, best advantage.

Giving Models for Lower-Income Groups

This book is not intended to dictate a totally precise model for any one person, but the numbers serve as a map leading to the important destination of good strategic planning, the forerunner to financial peace of mind.

Let's look now at how the financial situations of four income groups (ranging from averages of $85,000 to $590,000 in AGI) might fare after one, five, ten, twenty, and thirty years — and let's compare them to the average top-bracket wealth group, with its "assigned" donation level and other financial characteristics as discussed in Chapter 15). The approximate dollar and annualized percentage changes in inflation-adjusted earning assets that might be expected are shown in Table 8.

Table 8 Discussed

Based on the financial assumptions of the breakthroughs, Table 8 shows the estimated changes in earning-asset wealth after a reasonable amount of increased charitable contributions, and with all assigned donations receiving their related tax savings.

It is clear that the new assigned charitable donation potentials leave only the top ($16 million EA) group with virtually unchanged inflation-adjusted wealth after one- and five-year periods. The other four brackets are plus 3 to 8 percent per year over five years, and all groups are net positive, with healthy percentage in-

Table 8: Estimated Giving Effects for 1991's Top Five Tax-Bracket Groups
(assuming five years of raised donations followed by 1991 giving ratios)

Average AGI[a] and EA (in thousands)	Present-Value Earning Assets[b] (dollar figures in thousands)				
	After Year One	*After Year Five*	*After Year Ten*	*After Year Twenty*	*After Year Thirty*
AGI: $1,825	+0.81%	+0.83%	+2.29%	+2.97%	+3.17%
EA: $16,000	$16,129	$16,672	$20,063	$28,719	$40,847
AGI: $590	+2.89%	+2.82%	+3.53%	+3.70%	+3.67%
EA: $3,600	$3,704	$4,137	$5,093	$7,439	$10,614
AGI: $265	+4.13%	+3.98%	+4.33%	+4.20%	+4.01%
EA: $1,300	$1,354	$1,580	$1,987	$2,959	$4,225
AGI: $125	+5.94%	+5.66%	+5.80%	+5.31%	+4.89%
EA: $400	$424	$527	$703	$1,125	$1,677
AGI: $85	+8.51%	+7.88%	+7.57%	+6.66%	+5.87%
EA: $150	$163	$219	$311	$545	$829

NOTE: The next two lower-income brackets are not calculated, as they do not represent the ideal candidates for additional giving. Minor inconsistencies exist due to rounding of figures.
[a] Excluding capital gains.
[b] Percentages are annualized averages.

crements, for all subsequent time spans. Since the enhanced giving is assumed to end after five years, the long-term financial picture is positive for all. Note that I have allowed for a progressively greater relative net worth accumulation for the lower-wealth groups than for the higher ones for all periods. (If, however, percentage returns decline over the long run, as is the case in the $85,000 to $265,000 AGI categories, it is because they own fewer of the higher-return investments than the higher-wealth groups and because they suffer more tax bracket "creep" than those that start at higher levels).

To clarify Table 8's results, let's assume that Miranda Hill is the typical taxpayer who reports $125,000 in annual income and who has accumulated $400,000 in earning assets. Let's also assume that Ms. Hill is contemplating a big hike in the $3,000 she has been giving to charities each year — tripling her donation to, say, $9,000. How can she decide what effect this increase will have on her financial statement? How can she decide more intelligently on the affordability of her goals, and whether some small, carefully planned dipping into capital to accomplish them is advisable — or even necessary?

The answer lies in Ms. Hill's following the same breakthrough methodologies that led to the figures in Table 8. For example, she would estimate her total spending, including taxes. As the typical person in her tax bracket (see Table 2), she might have retained some 24 percent of her $125,000 income, or $30,000, after all expenses and taxes were paid. This $30,000 is the amount of discretionary income from which she could decide how to balance investing for the future, spending more on less-essential items, giving to family or charities, or the like.

But there are two other critical items to consider. First, she will want to know what is likely to happen with her $400,000 in investments. Although their current cash flow has been included in her $125,000 AGI, she will need to assess whether the assets themselves are rising in value or dropping. Second, she will want to account for inflation. She will want to quantify the likelihood of her increasing her "purchasing power" for possible emergencies, living extravagances, inheritance goals, and, yes, even possible philanthropic endeavors. So, she should follow the patterns explained earlier in the analysis of the highest-income earners, where income, spending, investment forecasts, and inflation have been accounted for — and where reasonable wealth figures can thus be estimated.

Table 8 shows a summary of the results. The $125,000-income row indicates that Ms. Hill's EA grew 5.94 percent in the first year, rising from $400,000 to $424,000. The $424,000 is adjusted for inflation of 3 percent; thus, the nominal wealth would be $437,000, but the actual purchasing power would be the $424,000 calculated above. Importantly, if she had kept her donations at $3,000, and instead used the additional $6,000 for a vacation trip (losing about $2,000 in tax deductions), her inflation-adjusted wealth would be $422,000, rather than $424,000.

What has the modeling done for Ms. Hill? It has given her a better perspective from which to budget her finances. It has allowed her to estimate better what her longer-term future might hold under changing circumstances of her choice. For example, Table 8 shows that five years of such tripled charitable contributions still leaves her with an inflation-adjusted average 5.66 percent *per year* more than her original capital. Her $400,000 in EA has grown to an inflation-adjusted $527,000. If she goes back to her prior average donations after five years and adjusts for inflation and a continuation of other factors, her ten-year total will be $703,000.

So Ms. Hill's vistas have been broadened. She has realistically assessed the most important financial considerations. She has included both income and asset values and has zeroed in on her spending essentials and other financial variables, as well as spending or gifting that could positively change her life.

As Breakthrough 5 revealed, the length of time that might be planned for spending on better living or for heightened giving should be varied according to financial position. Very wealthy people whose income and assets are well protected can think in terms of commitments even beyond five years, while those with either high risk of decrease or with low-to-medium wealth should plan on shorter horizons. Similarly, many people will enter different brackets over time and will need to reassess their levels as these changes occur.

Examples of Flexible JASS Thinking Applied to the Five Highest AGI/EA Groups' Assigned Charitable Donations

Table 8's figures suggest that our increased donation levels are affordable. Let's see now how the same donations sound in JASS methodology language. As the title of Table 9 states, I am now "converting calculations of charitable giving to both income and earning assets," with adjustments for the related tax deductions.

Table 9 Discussed

Column 1 includes the top bracket and the four lower (but not "low") categories. Column 2 shows the average reported charity donation for each bracket in 1991. Column 3 provides the "model" charitable donations — assigned, yet easily affordable,

Table 9: Converting Calculations of Charitable Giving to Both Income and Earning Assets and Allowing for Tax Deductions
(dollar figures in thousands)

	1	2	3	4	5	6	7	8
	1991 Reported AGI/ Earning Assets	1991 Reported Charity Donation	Model Charity Donation (Pretax)	Assigned After-Tax Cost of Donation		Remaining After-Tax Cost of Donation	
				Model Donation (After Tax)[a]	In Dollar Terms	As Percentage of AGI	In Dollar Terms	As Percentage of Earning Assets
$1,825/$16,000	$87.0	$900.0	$540.0	$360.0	19.7%	$180.0	1.13%
$ 590/$3,600	18.0	121.0	73.0	49.0	8.3%	24.0	0.67%
$ 265/$1,300	7.0	33.0	21.0	14.0	5.3%	7.0	0.54%
$ 125/$400	3.0	9.0	6.2	4.1	3.4%	2.1	0.52%
$ 85/$150	2.0	3.7	2.6	1.8	2.1%	0.8	0.53%

[a] Using varying marginal tax rates of different income brackets (from top down, respectively, 40, 40, 36, 31, and 28%, assuming federal taxes only).

levels for each group. And column 4 adjusts these donations for the approximate tax deductions that would occur with such gifts in 1994. Next I take the after-tax donation amount from column 4 and *arbitrarily* apportion some part of this figure to income; in Miranda Hill's $125,000/$400,000 (AGI/EA) case, two-thirds of the new $6,200 after-tax donation level has been "assigned" to income, and this $4,100 (column 5) amounts to approximately 3.4 percent (column 6) of her $125,000 income.

Columns 7 and 8 simply take what's left of the total donation and assign it to asset wealth (expressed as "Earning Assets"). In Ms. Hill's case, the remaining $2,100 amounts to 0.52 percent of her $400,000 of investments. So now she has a clearer picture of how affordable the $9,000 total gift was. Does 3.4 percent of income and one-half of 1 percent of EA (columns 6 and 7) sound onerous? You be the judge! Apportioning the giving this way provides a fairer statement of what Ms. Hill can and cannot do.

Table 9 also reiterates the small relative sacrifices suggested in this book. My hope is that, by this point, a 20 percent after-tax tithe on income (excluding capital gains) for the highest-earning group doesn't seem onerous; and that 1.13 percent of EA appears equally reasonable, provided that annual earning power and investment gains are sufficient to keep EA at reasonable inflation-adjusted levels. The same can, I hope, be said for the progressively lower allocations for those with smaller income and wealth, where EA goals are more demanding.

The assigned charitable donations could easily have been divided differently. Instead of arbitrarily assigning $360,000 of the highest-wealth group's $540,000 after-tax donation to a percentage of income, assume we had reversed the allocations and assigned $270,000 — in which case the income portion would have amounted to 15 percent while the share of earning assets would have amounted to 1.7 percent. The 15 percent of income amounts to only half of the estimated net "Available for Savings," column 6 of Table 2, for the top IRS grouping. And remember that no investment capital appreciation has been considered in these figures. The same philosophy applies to all groups. And the same affordable allocations to giving pertain for the five groupings of wealth indicated.

Some might argue that the top groups have sacrificed precious little compared to their relative wealth. This was "allowed" because my computer models for this book's purpose were driven by, among other things, a conservative limitation on corpus shrinkage owing to enhanced giving. Moreover, as mentioned, much larger donations become "more expensive" as certain income or wealth levels reach points where tax savings are no longer possible. Had I been less sensitive to the attractiveness of tax savings, or had I assumed that present-value earning assets could be reduced further without shocking readers, affordable giving from high-bracket individuals could have been increased — perhaps substantially. For example, had the $1.8 million earner with $16 million in EA been portrayed as a person with lower spending needs or with no inheritance requirements, and had the breakthrough spreadsheets been programmed to allow a drop in present-value assets to perhaps $15 million, the giving number would have increased to over $1,200,000 rather than $900,000 for each of the five years.

Greater empathy for the lower-bracket filers and lower-wealth owners is warranted, for obvious reasons. The assets of these groups are not allowed to shrink; in fact, they are encouraged to expand through far less demanding donations. It should be clear, too, that all of this is intended as an "order of magnitude" guide to a worthwhile outcome — and that living better (or at least not depriving yourself unnecessarily) can also be a more obtainable goal as a result of the *Wealthy and Wise* approach.

Chapter 18

Opportunities for Increased Giving by Foundations and Businesses

INDIVIDUALS aren't the only source of additional giving that could contribute substantially to the healing of America's problems. Two other groups could do more, too. Let's turn now to a closer look at the implications of our numerous breakthroughs for enhanced giving by charitable foundations and businesses.

Private and Community Foundations

Some organizations are already set up solely for charitable giving, especially those that make up the universe of private and community grantmaking foundations in the United States. Their funds emanate from a variety of sources and are donated by living individuals as well as those who transfer ownership of assets (with no taxation) at the time of death.

While such foundations can be found in different forms and sizes, many have substantial assets — a small portion of which are normally distributed to charities each year. Current tax laws reward foundations giving away 5 percent or more of their average corpus annually, and 5 percent is all that most contribute. For example, statistics from the Foundation Center in New York City for periods approximating 1992 listed 33,348 private and community major foundations in the United States, with year-end total assets of $162.9 billion. This cluster of funds made $9.2 billion in awards, or 5.6 percent of their year-end corpus.

Is 5.6 percent adequate? Isn't it practical, perhaps even wise, for foundations to consider an increase in their giving in this exceptional time of need?

Overseeing a foundation myself, and representing numerous others in my investment management business, I am sensitive to certain special conditions involving these vehicles. Many of these grantmakers possess no source of additional funds other than their residual income and any capital appreciation of their corpus. Many expect no further contributions from the outside, meaning that they rely mainly on their investments, which can certainly go down in value as well as up. Furthermore, most foundations have expenses to pay — staff and managerial costs, fees for attorneys, investment advisers and other specialists, rent and related expenses — while still keeping up with inflation. Consequently, many foundations are especially concerned about falling asset values and sharply rising inflation, such as occurred so dramatically in 1973 and 1974. These developments could be repeated and should never be forgotten.

Thus, many foundations are like retirees or others whose expenses exceed their income and who can count on stable net worth only through stable investment results. As such, the organizations are rightfully conservative, and generally view asset preservation as their only means to existence in the future.

Despite the fiscal realities, we cannot lose sight of the major philosophical mission of these bodies — which is, of course, to make wise, meaningful grants to good causes. People working for and with these entities are normally of the highest caliber. But, being human, they have the same fears and potential excuses (some rational, some not) that cause people to be extra conservative in their giving. A further complication may be that their personal interests may be tied to perpetuating the entities they represent. In addition, many foundations are set up to exist in perpetuity with limitations on money available for grants. In short, there are good reasons for them to conclude that they "simply can't afford" to give more — regardless of the organization's asset growth.

Table 10: Foundation Asset and Gift Statistics, 1992
(dollar figures in thousands)

1	2	3	4	5	6	7	8	9
Average Corpus	Gifts Received	Estimated Income Earned[a]	Estimated Capital Gains[a]	Estimated Total Additions	Grants Paid Out	Operating Expenditures	Total Payouts	Net Loss
$4,885	$164	$220	$171	$555	$276	$334	$610	($55)

These figures follow in percentage terms:

100.0%	3.4%	4.5%	3.5%	11.4%	5.6%	6.8%	12.5%	(1.1%)

[a] Based on an estimated equal ownership of bonds and common stocks, with an assumed 4.5% annual income (6.5% and 2.5% respectively) and with capital gains estimated at 7% for stocks only.
SOURCE: The Foundation Center, New York City.

Yet the model for increasing individual giving and delicate dipping applies to the foundation world as well. Table 10 foundation statistics (see above) provide an opportunity to conduct the same kind of affordability analysis as that used for individuals. The table sets forth important data pertaining to the 33,348 major foundations with year-end assets of $162.9 billion. All amounts shown are actual except those in columns 3, 4, and 5, where I have estimated income and capital appreciation of assets since they were not specifically reported by the Foundation Center.

Table 10 Discussed

Many foundations receive no additional assets — yet column 2 shows that the average fund received $164,000 from the outside in that period. Operating costs (column 7) ran $334,000, or 6.8 percent of the average corpus — a figure that seems especially high for a $4.9 million entity that made average grants of $276,000 (column 6). And column 9 indicates that in a normal investment year with a diversified portfolio of bonds and stocks, the corpus might have ended the year at $55,000, or a slim 1.1 percent below the prior year's total.

This negative cash flow obviously provides no cushion for inflation protection; hence, there doesn't seem to be much, if any, room for additional giving. In the case of many foundations, therefore, funds for greater giving would have to come directly from their earning assets. Is this reckless?

The answer is yes — if you look at this one year alone. Looking further back, which is what should be done, the picture changes. Given the exceptional returns earned from bonds and stocks over the past ten to fifteen years, it's logical to assume that neither foundation founders nor trustees ever dreamed that their inflation-adjusted asset levels would ever come close to what exists today. Considering this along with their purpose to fill needs and improve society, shouldn't foundations engage in a conservative program to give more than the legally required minimum? The urgency is there, what with the problems and the inability of the government to fill the gaps. So why not commence a program of delicate dipping into capital similar to that suggested for certain (mainly wealthy) individuals?

For example, giving a supplemental 1 or 2 percent of corpus to annual giving over the next half-decade amounts to less than 5 to 10 percent of present-value reduction of capital. Based on recent asset values, this 1 to 2 percent would constitute an additional $1.63 billion to $3.25 billion per year on a static $163 billion foundation base. And these prospects are understated, since the list of foundations is not all-inclusive.

Finally, foundations are permitted to include certain of their costs in their giving totals. Substituting grants for a reduction of these internal costs is another source of greater philanthropy.

Corporations and Businesses

Corporations and businesses obviously have goals that are very different from foundations. While most businesses would like to believe that they provide some social benefit, the primary motivation of most is to make money. In fact, many businesses resist distributing even small portions of profits to charities. In publicly traded companies, or even in private companies with diverse ownership, there are those who insist that the profits belong solely to the shareholders. If, they contend, the shareholders wish to make contributions from their dividends or from stock appreciation, that is their business; but they do not believe the organization itself should make such decisions for them. The case of large corporations likewise poses problems for some, including economist John Kenneth Galbraith, who contends that increased corporate giving only leads to further opportunities for giant organizations to exercise undue influence.

Government policy, however, fosters corporate giving, with an allowable 10 percent of taxable income considered deductible as a result of the Economic Recovery Tax Act (ERTA) of 1981. (For the preceding forty-six years, the limit had been 5 percent.) The 1981 Task Force on Private Sector Initiatives flatly encouraged charitable support by businesses; this task force reiterated a prior commission's recommendation that "by 1986, every company in the U.S., large or small, [should] give 2 percent of pretax net income to nonprofit organizations engaged in public service."

Legal precedents likewise encourage higher corporate giving. In 1953, the New Jersey Supreme Court ruled that "corporations not only had the right to make contributions, they also had a duty to do so as a matter of social responsibility" (*Smith Manufacturing v. Barlow*).

It shouldn't be a surprise that my personal bias favors businesses shouldering responsibilities that go far beyond making profits. Pressing local, civic, and national needs exist, and it seems logical that these burdens be considered as part of the community responsibility of commercial enterprises. Businesses certainly have significant economic incentives to contribute; their tax rates are generally higher than individual levies and they can obtain the appropriate write-offs. Businesses are normally in a symbiotic relationship with the community in which they operate. And, of course, a better-educated, "better-behaved" work force constitutes a strong foundation for business success. As a New York–based business roundtable stated: "How well we educate all of our children will determine our competitiveness globally and our economic health domestically." Hence, corporate sharing is more than an obligation. Properly directed, the sharing produces benefits for the shareholders. As McKesson Corporation's Marvin L.

Krasnanski wrote to *Pensions and Investments Age*, "The CEO's job is to make sure the business succeeds, but a business cannot succeed if society fails."

Yet the facts about business giving are confusing. Although post-ERTA data indicate that corporations have contributed slightly less than 2 percent of pretax profits, privately held businesses have not been part of the studies, and the focus has been almost exclusively on the largest publicly held companies. For example, the 1991 *Corporate Giving Directory* (published by the Taft Group of Rockville, Maryland) presented profiles of America's major corporate foundations' charitable-giving programs. The 478 names on the Taft list contributed $2.1 billion in 1988, or an average of $4.4 million per company. Since the group included so many of the Fortune 500, this $4.4 million hardly seemed "aggressive." So, what percentage of profits did these donations represent?

The results were startling. Although I pared the 478 names down to 304 because numerous companies were privately held or because their earnings were not in data bases owing to mergers and for other reasons, these 304 corporations actually had donated 88 percent of the total amount. Here are the data.

1988 pretax net income of the 304	$216.79 billion
1988 charitable gifts from the group	$1.85 billion
Giving as a percentage of pretax profits	0.85%

Although it is possible that this compilation may be understated because of in-kind contributions and volunteerism (employees "loaned" to charitable organizations, for example), independently wealthy individuals also obviously volunteer and claim no monetary donations for this. Furthermore, many corporations can count donations of company products as charitable donations when in fact they qualify equally as sales promotion. A case in point is a very profitable computer manufacturer that one year listed its charitable contributions at $8.5 million; of this, $8.0 million was in hardware given to schools and organizations that were large potential buyers or that influenced many users of their products in the future. An insignificant $0.5 million was sent to charities in cash.

A legitimate rationale for the modest donations is the difficult times experienced by corporate America from the mid- to late 1980s on. While more cost cutting is in store, industry by industry our businesses are becoming more competitive in global markets in terms of both quality and price. Ultimately, this should lead to strong profitability — at which time countless companies will, I hope, raise their levels of giving in a meaningful way. A hike in giving to a mere 2 or 3 percent (which amounts to 1.3 to 2.0 percent after taxes) would produce a hefty annual increase to worthy causes: some $2.5 billion to 4.7 billion per year (at 1988 levels). And this is from a tiny sample of 304 companies. The potential for increased giving from the business community is obviously substantial. As a matter of fact, companies such as Ben & Jerry's, Dayton Hudson, H. B. Fuller, and Levi Strauss (and probably many more) already allocate giving in a range of 2.5 to 5 percent of pretax income. Then there is actor Paul Newman's food company, which contributes even higher amounts to charity and has already allocated over $80 million to such causes.

It is hard to believe that an annual allotment of an incremental 1 or 2 percent of net income after taxes would make businesses less competitive to overseas competition, or that this would entail a sacrifice sufficient to harm shareholders. Positive benefits would include better employee relations, perhaps better prepared and better trained staff, and an improved public image from whatever social improvements emanate from larger and wiser giving.

If nothing else, solving infrastructure and other societal problems will result in an improved social climate and a brighter future that in turn will positively affect business. The inevitability of higher taxation for businesses (as well as for wealthy individuals) if problems are not solved is also a strong reason for higher giving.

But there are additional, practical reasons, too. Reaching Out giving by foundations and corporations would demonstrate the leadership they can provide to the country. They need to become stronger advocates of philanthropy; they need to improve their judgment of what to support; they need to show nonprofits how to manage themselves better. They could magnify their employees' donations through matching-gift programs and encouraged volunteerism, and much more. A fine example of coordinated, cooperative giving of this sort is San Francisco's annual Christmas in April

campaign, described earlier, in which businesses directly contribute money, supplies, and direction, and encourage their employees to add their own labor and support — to complete needed
construction-type projects at mere fractions of what they would
otherwise cost. Finally, the impact from concentrated donations
by businesses that can realize greater efficiencies from the recipients is obviously superior to the same money coming from a series
of smaller, passive gifts. Indeed, the potential from businesses is
substantial and relatively untapped.

Chapter 19

Propitious Timing for Using Your Capital

STOCK market wizard Bernard Baruch once observed that the most appropriate time for consumers to buy straw hats is decidedly in the winter, when retailers do not have eager buyers and when they probably have to mark down their prices to eliminate inventory. From the retailers' standpoint, however, the appropriate time to sell these items is in the hottest months, when buyers might need them desperately and might be willing to pay premium prices. Baruch's principle — sell straw hats in the summer if you're a retailer and buy them in the winter if you're a consumer — contains some parallels with the thesis of this book.

What exactly does this have to do with more comfortable living or increased charitable giving and the plea for individuals, foundations, and corporations to reconsider their present policies? How does Baruch's analogy regarding bargains and values relate to this new definition of surplus money and increasing affordable donations?

Given the robust returns earned by financial assets from 1975 through 1993, Baruch's adage is a reminder that shifting the earnings from bonds or common stocks to increased giving or better-living expenditures at the present time might be propitious. This suggestion, made earlier but worth expanding, is not intended to make a specific forecast for stocks, bonds, or any other investment vehicles.

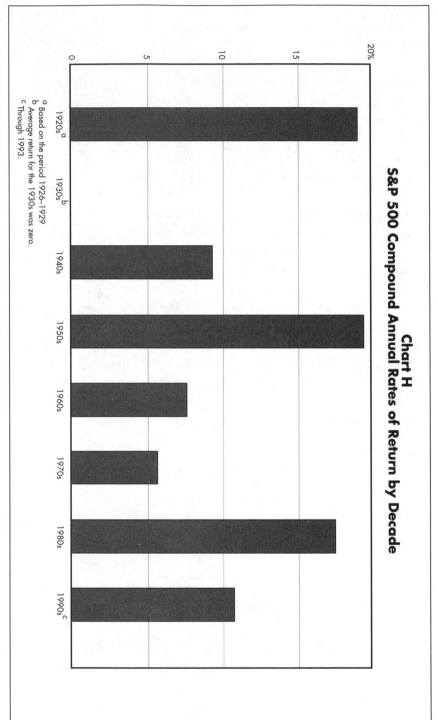

Chart H
S&P 500 Compound Annual Rates of Return by Decade

a Based on the period 1926–1929
b Average return for the 1930s was zero.
c Through 1993.

Chart A (page 29) shows clearly how common stocks and bonds have produced extremely positive results in recent years. Compound total returns (income plus capital appreciation) for the Standard & Poor 500 Stock Index amounted to 14.3 percent annually for the thirteen years 1981 to 1993, while total returns on US Treasury bonds were well above average. Powerful results such as these have occurred before, but as Chart H shows, the normal pattern has been for returns exceeding 10 percent to be followed by inferior results; similar conclusions can be made about bonds, which are offering their lowest income yields in more than two decades.

Profitable results such as these should not be ignored. To duplicate or better this recent experience would suggest a new era of heightened prosperity. Optimists will point to the prospects from the surge in the new market economies of the Eastern bloc, the Far East, and Latin America, the downfall of communism, the welcome conversion of a large proportion of US military spending to more productive outlets, the North American Free Trade Agreement's lowering of trade barriers, plus the strong positive profit leverage that exists in American industry today under moderately improved volume and pricing conditions. On the other hand, there are the already-mentioned negatives of infrastructure problems and governmental deficits, plus sharply higher wage levels in the United States in comparison to those enjoyed by a growing number of competitors, as well as the usual international political and military instabilities.

Investors should also consider the base level of fundamentals that currently support common stocks. As of early 1994, the stock market was priced higher in relation to reported stock earnings, dividend yields, and book value than it was in most other stellar performing periods. If business is to make a strong recovery and these fundamentals are to increase, there is certainly room for continued favorable returns from stocks — especially if inflation is slow enough to allow interest rates to remain at moderate levels or to decline.

Still, there are reasons to suggest that cashing in a few chips here and there is at least prudent and could possibly prove to be very wise. And this is where the Baruch principle comes in.

Shouldn't potential contributors sell or donate — particularly in a way where capital gains taxes can be avoided — at least some portion of their "straw hats" in what statistically seems to be a part of an investment summer season?

For the record, these suggestions do not emanate from a pessimist or a doomsayer. I have long been an optimist about equity investing and definitely feel that long-term investors will prosper handsomely. But my pragmatic side also suggests that there will eventually be an interruption in the euphoric conditions that have prevailed in stocks for so long now.

It is wise to learn from the past. For example, I will never forget the traumas that were faced by a broad spectrum of investors in 1974. A good friend and most competent administrator, Roger Kennedy, was then financial vice president of the Ford Foundation. Roger called me in the fall of 1974. A leader in the charitable-foundation world, he sensed the near-panic being experienced at other foundations. Assets were declining sharply on a nominal basis, and with inflation running rampant, the results were frightening.

Kennedy thought it essential to talk to other leaders in his field, to discuss whether the investment world was slated for further disaster and, particularly, to calm fears about permanent disappointments. Roger asked me if I would speak to a number of groups, which I agreed to do. The problems seemed quite solvable, and Kennedy and I determined that we might save these institutions from liquidating their portfolios at or near market bottoms. Fortunately, few if any of the institutions panicked, and literally billions of dollars were saved.

Today's condition is quite the reverse of the fall of 1974. Prices are high. Returns have been great. It certainly seems prudent and plausible to maximize some gains and shift at least small portions of these heightened assets to societal improvement. Indeed, since there is a need for capital to fund a turnaround of our problems, it is completely sensible to transfer some of this investment good fortune into important causes.

Chapter 20

Attractive Options for the Wealthy

TOO many people relegate the all-important charitable giving considerations of "how much," "when," and "to whom" to the bottom of their priority lists and never even consider a variety of attractive government-sanctioned options that exist, especially for high-bracket taxpayers.

Of course, regulations are always subject to change, and vehicles that are tax effective today may not be so in the future. That's why this book is not the place to specify the best options for any person or circumstance. Still, you should be well informed about the techniques and the possibilities, as you should understand that efficient management of your assets while you are alive is often best accompanied by proper planning for their distribution upon your death.

So let's explore some broad principles that might help you with your planning. For example, special charitable trusts allow donors to

- benefit from reductions of ordinary income, capital gains, and inheritance taxes;
- use low cost-basis assets for the gifts;
- retain, and in many cases substantially increase, a specific amount of income from the gifted assets, either for designated periods or for life; and
- possibly even allow the assets to be invaded during the donor's lifetime.

Other vehicles provide income to charities while the donor is alive and can benefit from related tax deductions, and then allow the assets to flow to designated heirs at death.

Plans such as these can smooth the path to giving, particularly for those who want to be extra certain that they haven't lost a source of income that might be needed later on. These mechanisms, as well as the use of community funds and other foundations, can also alleviate worries about control of donations after death.

Take the case of two brothers I knew who were lifetime business partners. One, Frank, lived into his nineties and found that his favorite and most productive interest during his final thirty years came from donating money and giving time to his favorite charities. His brother, Don, was not so lucky. His life span was ten years shorter than Frank's, and he had spent most of his last twenty years worrying unnecessarily about his assets and husbanding his ample wealth. He chose to spend his resources on neither personal pleasures nor charities while he lived, although he did leave money to a new family foundation upon his death.

I met Frank and Don's sister Evelyn at a luncheon one day, and when another guest raised the subject of money and enjoyment, the sister compared the lives of her brothers, concluding that Frank's was productive and happy while Don's was relatively unhappy and lacked both purpose and proper planning. A former attorney, the sister lamented that Don was foolish to hoard his money and shortsighted not to have formed one of the attractive options mentioned above: in this case, a supporting foundation.

"A supporting foundation," she explained, "could have changed Don's life. Beyond its tax deductibility, it could have provided him with a productive, yet inexpensive, outlet. He could have formed the foundation and could have designated individuals, including his children, to participate actively along with him in philanthropic grants awarded while he was alive."

Evelyn's regrets went a lot further than lost tax deductions and unattained pleasures. She was also upset over how Don's heirs, his appointed new foundation trustees, were parceling out donations from the enterprise. She was angry that the contributions weren't to "important" causes. "Sadly, they didn't cover any areas that Don would have been proud of," she said. "To think how simple it would have been for him to establish a philanthropic habit while he lived, to direct money where it would have given him the greatest satisfaction, perhaps to receive immediate recognition for his generosity and maybe even to train his children in the art of giving efficiently, all the while retaining the assets in a foundation set aside to provide the income for his gifts." Evelyn concluded that Don had "wasted a great opportunity."

Wasted opportunity, indeed. Don could have engaged in painless giving while alive. He could have provided better for both his community's and his family's future. And he could have recommended either broad or specific targets for his foundation grants after his demise. He could have taken advantage of the attributes provided by a supporting foundation, a charitable remainder or an annuity unitrust, or similar options, one of which was recently described to me: a friend of mine waxed eloquently to me how he had "just achieved the best of both worlds," through a large gift made to his alma mater. He had wanted to honor his deceased wife, whose compelling interest had been in child counseling. A building was uppermost among his choices, but the price tag for this was almost $5 million. Although he had assets that greatly exceeded this amount, practically all of his wealth resided in a common stock that paid no cash dividends, thereby keeping his income low. His ability to compensate for this was hampered by the zero cost-basis of the stock, which meant that selling it entailed paying more than one-third of the value in capital gains taxes.

The happy medium for him was "deferred giving," which involved several simple steps. First, he transferred $5 million of his stock into a charitable trust. In this case, the trustees sold the stock, and since it was liquidated within the trust, there were no capital gains taxes due. Next, the trustees reinvested the proceeds from the sale into a solid, income-producing entity. Importantly, the trustees divided this new property into two parts. He retained the first part, which was an interest in the income from the trust throughout his lifetime, while agreeing that the school would receive the second part, which was all the trust's assets at the time of his death. In exchange for this, the university agreed to construct (immediately) a new counseling center named for his late wife.

So, my friend now had a new source of significant and potentially growing income, plus a more diversified net worth. He also received a tax deduction for his gift (not based on the full $5 million, but on a portion of it adjusted for the amount of income he was to take from the trust during his lifetime, and further adjusted for an actuarial estimate of his remaining life span). It's also possible, depending on the trust's investments, that part of the income he receives might be treated as capital gains and taxed at a lower rate, or possibly as a tax-free return of principal. And, of course, he gained the satisfaction of the gift itself, of what he provided for posterity in his wife's name.

Fortunately, you don't have to be wealthy to accomplish efficient ways of giving as described above. Charitable-gift mutual funds that are the equivalents of public charities welcome small investment accounts. Your contributions are tax deductible and are invested as they might be in any mutual fund. In this case the income and any capital appreciation accumulates without taxation, and you can designate checks in certain minimum amounts to charities of your choice for as long as your account exists. There are also community charities and other philanthropically driven institutions that accomplish similar objectives, with generally lower costs and fewer restrictions to the investor/donor.

As these few examples make clear, there are numerous attractive options that should encourage far greater participation in philanthropy.

Chapter 21

Getting Smarter About Your Giving

REACHING OUT expanded giving is legitimized, first, by America's critical needs and, second, by the proof that it is affordable. Its insistence on more forceful leadership is justified by increasing obstacles from governments, bureaucracies, special-interest groups, and even certain nonprofits themselves.

As with many other pursuits, gifting wisely requires thought. Regardless of the size of your donation or your allocated time as a volunteer, you deserve to feel confident that your chosen nonprofits have the capabilities to carry out their missions efficiently. There are questions to ask and information to gather to make yourself a smarter judge of nonprofits and a happier contributor to them. Let's start with some general advice.

1. Start with your values — philanthropy is based on values. Rank your priorities. Zero in on your most passionate interest. Is it youth or the elderly? Local needs versus national or global? Environment, education, public policy, the arts? Make a list and keep track of how you hope to allocate your dollars and time.

2. Do your homework on the issues. Are the needs that strike you as critical truly so dire? Perhaps they are already being met. Perhaps ample funding is already available.

3. Develop a philanthropic plan — an organized strategy.

4.   Concentrate your efforts and donations and your involvement. You will wear yourself out thrusting in a multitude of directions, and your attitude may suffer accordingly. I had just such an experience when I first entered the business world in the mid-1950s. Without proper planning, I became a member of five nonprofit organizations, and I soon found myself resentful of the time their meetings were taking. This resentment then turned into criticism of the organizations — until one day I recognized they were not at fault at all. I was! I was spread so thin I couldn't give much to any one of them, so neither I nor the groups were benefiting. Eventually I narrowed my focus and worked hard for two organizations; this proved successful for both them and me. Concentrating your monetary donations by targeting certain charities can also lead to success. If you become particularly important to an institution, you stand a far better chance of influencing decisions and helping it to achieve its mission.

5.   Isolate the potential obstacles that might hamper the organization's success. Ask its leaders what they perceive these obstacles to be. (Beware if they expect none.) Then assess the group's abilities to overcome the roadblocks. Remember that the most efficient Reaching Out may require firmness and even tough bargaining. You should determine whether a group has the fortitude to buck obstacles, move beyond setbacks, and foster change.

6.   Don't be bashful about asking tough questions of the charitable organizations you are assessing. In my book *Investing with the Best*, I recommend that people who are seeking investment help ask what I term "impertinent questions" of potential advisers. Impertinent in this case does not mean impolite, but it does mean penetrating. The analogy when assessing nonprofits is to request information on items such as executive and staff compensation, including perks; payments, if any, to directors or trustees (including any business directed to them); entertainment and related expenses incurred; numbers of volunteers and hours worked by them; numbers of paid workers and their salary levels; total administrative expenses in relation to program dollars spent; and even the amount of in-kind donations received (these will presumably lower overhead expense ratios). Do *not* rely on anecdotes supplied by the organizations. Force them into supplying specifics. As

Ira Hirschfield of the Evelyn and Walter Haas Jr. Fund demands, "Tell me how you *know* what you are doing is working."

Try also to quantify the nonprofit's accomplishments and the costs of obtaining those results. For example, determine the number of people helped and to what degree, and then assess the organization's costs to make this happen (say, through a per-person-helped or similar ratio).

7. As in business, nonprofits undertake projects with near-term and long-term horizons. Ask the organization to separate its goals into time periods, and then track the results. Probe why the near-term goals have not been met; and be patient, but press for progress reports on those earmarked for the future.

8. Study the organization's past accomplishments and relate them to the dollars spent. Did the group achieve what you would expect? Financial position is important. Funds may be needed, but an organization should not be so strapped that it is likely to fail in its mission.

9. Of course, you can always insist that your donation be directed only to a specific project; in fact, you can even make your pledge contingent on some specifically defined successful conclusion. Similarly, if you are a large donor, you might consider leveraging your gift with either a "challenge" or a "matching" grant. The former motivates the nonprofit to attain a certain total sum from other contributors: unless the prescribed total is reached, your donation may be withheld. With a matching gift, you may set a ratio of your potential donation to an amount to be raised elsewhere by the nonprofit; for example, you might require that one or two dollars of others' money be raised for every dollar of yours, up to some stated maximum.

Here are some other examples of financial probing — simple financial lessons to prepare you to make better choices when you screen nonprofits.

Assessing the "Financials" of Nonprofits

Determine what the organization of your focus can afford to do and whether it is doing it efficiently. Unfortunately, this is not an exact science, and nonprofit accounting rules are not as well

formulated as those for profit-oriented businesses. One can hope
that the American Institute of Certified Public Accountants will
tighten its rules soon. Until then, here are three prudent rules of
thumb to use when you screen nonprofits.

- Do not accept any one ratio of effectiveness as the gospel.
  Ask numerous questions like those already listed.
- Treat any one ratio that seems improper as a serious cause
  for concern.
- Look elsewhere if an organization refuses to supply
  information.

Let's turn to a few basics that parallel the approaches recommended when analyzing personal affordability. In fact, it may be
more informative to judge nonprofit financial strengths and weaknesses, and organizations' abilities to deliver services at reasonable
costs, by adapting portions of my JASS (judging affordable spending
sensibly) methodology. You know how myopic it is to base affordability on income alone, how important it is to add net worth into
the equation, and how meaningful it is to break your donation potential into two parts that you then compare separately to income
and net worth. Well, you can follow a similar procedure in your
analysis of a charitable institution. The techniques to be learned
from the following example are simple to accomplish on your own.

Example: The XYZ Charitable Organization

XYZ's donations received during 1993	$1,000,000
Less expenses of fund-raising	200,000
Net donations received	$ 800,000
Amount retained of funds raised	$800,000 ÷ $1,000,000 = 80%

What have you learned by this simple calculation?

First, on average you can figure that 80 percent of your donation will probably end up in the XYZ coffers — a figure most commonly used to compare effectiveness against other nonprofits.
Frankly, the ratio is overemphasized, since it doesn't tell you how
much of your donation will be put to work or how effectively it will

be used. Keeping in mind the first and second of the three caveats just provided, I conclude that if the expenses of raising money are low, I still have some homework to do; but if they are high (say, over 20 percent), I need a good explanation why I should not look elsewhere.

Let's shift now to XYZ's capital funds, generally termed the organization's "endowment," and the investment income being earned from this source.

XYZ's Endowment Fund, December 31, 1993	$2,000,000
Income received from endowment investments	100,000
Total earning assets and income	$2,100,000
Now identify XYZ's 1993 program spending	$100,000
Apply the JASS method and divide this into	
two equal parts	$50,000
	50,000
Divide the first $50,000 portion of	
spending by XYZ's net donations	
(calculated above)	$50,000 ÷ $800,000 = 0.0625, or 6.25%
Divide the second portion of spending	
by XYZ's combined endowment and	
investment income	$50,000 ÷ $2,100,000 = 0.024, or 2.4%

Dividing the spending in half as we have, only 6.25 percent of the organization's donations has been used, plus 2.4 percent of its endowment fund. And the total spending of $100,000 amounts to 3.4 percent of the combined $2,000,000 endowment, $100,000 investment income, and $800,000 in net donations. Pretty skimpy, I'd say!

Incidentally, annual reports of many charitable organizations do not list the endowment funds held. Do not be bashful about requesting this or other information (including, in rare cases, copies of the organization's tax filings). To repeat the prior warning, if they won't supply informative reports, look elsewhere. If you are still curious, or if you want to test the entity's honesty, you can capitalize its income much as I capitalized AGI to arrive at the earning-asset wealth of individuals. In XYZ's case, had the $100,000 in earned income not been accompanied by endowment size, an estimated 5 percent income return would have given you a $2 million net worth projection ($100,000 divided by 0.05 equals $2 million).

You should also judge other efficiencies. Specific compensation of nonprofit management can be a clue to waste, fraud, or looseness of cost controls in any institution. While the exception, there have been examples of excessive compensation and other inefficiencies in nonprofits that could have been discovered early on. All anyone had to do was ask specific questions (for the third time; if incomplete responses were forthcoming, money should have been withheld). A cash flow analysis of the nonprofit's past year and its budget for the current one are also revealing statements for you to peruse.

Measurement is, of course, not only financial. To repeat, you should develop qualitative judgments that help you determine whether nonprofits are accomplishing their goals effectively and more successfully than others in the same fields.

All of the above is intended to make you a more careful and skillful contributor — to prepare you to take control of a process that is frequently out of control. After all, most philanthropy is based on a reaction to someone, often important to you, who may not know whether his or her chosen nonprofit truly produces good value relative to its funds. You are parting with money and you owe it to yourself (and perhaps even owe it to the government that allows you tax deductions for charitable donations) to strive for effectiveness. You are entitled to know that your dollars or your time are likely to be successfully deployed.

Chapter 22

Providing Adequately for Your Heirs

WHILE charitable gifts at death are currently free of taxation, property left to heirs is heavily taxed by the federal government and some states. Once the lifetime $600,000 personal exemption has been used, bequests to individuals other than a spouse are taxed as much as 55 to 60 percent. Hence, in planning for the inevitable, people have to realize that they may need approximately $1 million in assets in order to bequeath a total of $500,000 to their heirs, $10 million to $12 million to leave $5 million, and so forth.

The subject of bequests to heirs is a personal and delicate matter. Some people assume that everything should be passed on to their children, others plan for whatever their definition is of "moderation," and still others believe that almost anything left to young people is actually injurious to them.

Andrew Carnegie was of the latter belief, stating that fortunes left to children were "misguided affection," and that "it is not well for the children that they should be so burdened." He even went so far as to say, "I would as soon leave to my son a curse as the almighty dollar."

A September 1986 *Fortune* magazine article ("Should You Leave It All to Your Children?") offered some interesting insights. Interviews of successful people centered on their plans for passing assets to their children. Most were highly skeptical of leaving large sums, and some actually believed that virtually zero was the right number.

Psychologist John Levy of Mill Valley, California, provides a different, more constructive thought. Although he, too, worries about the guilt and "meaninglessness of life" that affect many recipients of inherited wealth, Levy suggests at least a partial fringe benefit: philanthropy. "With almost no exceptions," he says, "inheritors who come from families where philanthropy is valued as a central part of life turn out to be much better off [emotionally and psychologically] than those who don't." In Levy's experience, an active participatory role in charities by heirs can provide a meaningful offset to the adjustments that many face in their lives.

What to leave to heirs and how to prepare them for a bequest is a topic of great significance. Intelligent financial planning demands that all major obstacles and contingencies be considered. The desire to leave enough for others is often a barrier to individuals' comfortable living and to charitable giving while they are alive. The less money people have, the more difficult it will be for them to provide for basic living essentials or educational advantages for their heirs, and the more cautious they must be. Yet, as this book shows, delicate withdrawals from abundant capital do not endanger reasonable bequeathal goals.

An Organized, Sensible Way to Plan Bequests

Most people of means have well-constructed wills and trusts set up to accomplish their purposes. The usual caveat given them by their advisers is to "keep in touch" and to update these documents as circumstances change. The problem is that time flies by, and too often reassessments are neglected. To offset this, people may want to explore a will that adjusts automatically in response to at least two important variables: asset value of the estate and loss of purchasing power.

As with levels of giving and standards of living, bequests can be well planned. The procedures that follow can help accomplish this.

1. If you are married, discuss inheritance desires with your spouse, listing people you wish to remember. Differentiate be-

tween those who are to receive bequests as soon as one of you dies and those who are to be remembered only when you both are gone.

2. List all your assets, including eventual life insurance proceeds, at today's approximate market values; estimate and include any income you expect to be generated by these assets after your death.

Then, one excellent way to decide how much to leave to heirs is to consider (a) how much corpus might be needed by them for capital investments, including housing, and (b) how much capital might be needed to produce the level of annual income you want them to receive from your bequest. Remember, however, that certain assets that produce little or no current income predeath may be liquidated and converted to income producers after you die.

3. Visualize conditions with each spouse separately deceased. There is usually one major breadwinner, and analyzing what, if anything, is to be passed on to heirs normally depends on which spouse dies first.

4. Now visualize what happens if you die simultaneously. Decide how much is to be left to whom if you both were to die tomorrow.

5. Finally, decide which charities are to be remembered upon your death and in what approximate amounts, and consider establishing foundations or other vehicles to accomplish your goals propitiously.

In other words, there should be three lists: (1) Person A gone and person B the survivor; (2) person B gone and person A alive; and (3) person A and person B both deceased. This points to the construction of three spreadsheets, each listing the names of all possible heirs and obligations, along with approximate *percentage* allocations to each under the three conditions. Remember that the laws currently allow tax-free transfer of assets among spouses upon the death of one, and that the percentages used here for legacies in the event of death of just one spouse assume that each spouse's share of the estate consists of approximately half the assets owned. Consider the "Sample Prep Sheet" shown on page 154.

Sample Prep Sheet for Estate Planning: Designated Percentage Bequests

Possible beneficiaries if major income contributor (Spouse A) dies first		Possible beneficiaries if minor income contributor (Spouse B) dies first		Possible beneficiaries if spouses die simultaneously	
Spouse B	80.0%	Spouse A	70%	Child A	30.0%
Child A	7.5	Child A	10	Child B	30.0
Child B	7.5	Child B	10	Trusts for potential grandchildren	10.0
Sister A	1.0	Cousin B	2	Sister A	1.0
Brother A	1.0	Friend B	2	Brother A	1.0
Mother A and Father A	2.0	Brother B	2	Brother B	1.0
Charity	1.0	Charity	4	Mother A	2.5
				Father A	2.5
				Cousin B	1.0
				Friend B	1.0
				Charity	20.0

What's missing is the approximate dollar size of the estate. We now need spreadsheets that combine portions of the above information as column headings at the top, along with rows down the left-hand side of the page that cover all practical asset amounts (dollars) that might exist at death.

To illustrate, let's assume a less complicated list of heirs and obligations and concentrate on the third condition, both spouses deceased. Assume that Mr. and Mrs. Smith are considering their eventual deaths. They have $1.8 million in earnings and their $16 million in earning assets becomes $17 million with life insurance proceeds and $20 million with the value of homes, possessions, and so forth. They decide that their two children will be very adequately covered in today's terms with an inheritance of $3 million to each. (Assuming an evenly balanced bond/stock portfolio in 1994 values, this would produce an approximate $150,000 annual income to each beneficiary; capital appreciation from stocks over long periods might produce another $100,000 annually, bringing total returns to around $250,000 per year.)

The Smiths' will should state clearly that the specific inheritance intentions listed are to be adjusted for inflationary impacts in the future. Hence, the $3.0 million bequests to each child are to be increased, for example, by any future changes in the government's Consumer Price Index or some comparable inflation index.

The Smiths must remember, too, that each $3 million necessitates around $6 million in assets—let's assume 50 percent will be eliminated through inheritance taxes. Hence taxes will take $6 million, the two children will receive a total of $6 million, and there will thus be an $8 million remainder for other purposes.

Prioritizing inheritance is critical. The prep sheet allows the Smiths to decide whether charities will participate from the beginning with the children, or whether the couple will start with loved ones and favor charity only after the children's share has reached certain levels. The latter approach is used in the following example. Table 11 presents a spreadsheet for the first $12 million of this $20 million estate, with the guidelines already discussed (for simplicity's sake, the tax rate is evenly set at 50 percent for all levels).

So the first $12 million provides $3 million to each child,

Table 11: Smith Inheritance Allotments ($1 million to $12 million in assets)
(Date: January 3, 1994. Table to be adjusted for U.S. Government C.P.I.)

| Combined Assets (in millions) | Inheritance Percentages Directed to | | | | Inheritance Dollars Received by | | | | Inheritance Taxes Paid | Total Received by Heirs and Charity |
| | Taxed Heirs | | Nontaxed Recipients | | Taxed Heirs[a] Cumulative Amounts (in millions) | | Nontaxed Recipients | | | |
	Child 1	Child 2	Charity A	Charity B	Child 1	Child 2	Charity A	Charity B		
$ 1	50%	50%	0	0	$0.25	$0.25	0	0	$0.5	$0.5
2	50	50	0	0	0.50	0.50	0	0	1.0	1.0
3	50	50	0	0	0.75	0.75	0	0	1.5	1.5
4	50	50	0	0	1.00	1.00	0	0	2.0	2.0
5	50	50	0	0	1.25	1.25	0	0	2.5	2.5
6	50	50	0	0	1.50	1.50	0	0	3.0	3.0
7	50	50	0	0	1.75	1.75	0	0	3.5	3.5
8	50	50	0	0	2.00	2.00	0	0	4.0	4.0
9	50	50	0	0	2.25	2.25	0	0	4.5	4.5
10	50	50	0	0	2.50	2.50	0	0	5.0	5.0
11	50	50	0	0	2.75	2.75	0	0	5.5	5.5
12	50	50	0	0	3.00	3.00	0	0	6.0	6.0

[a] Tax rate of 50%.

for a total of $6 million — and with nothing yet earmarked for charity.

The question now is: How do the Smiths wish to divide the remaining $8 million? None to the children? All to charity? Parts to each? Assuming that the goal of $3 million to each child is properly stated in the will to be adjusted upward for future inflation (but no more than this), the rest of the spreadsheet will look like Table 12.

"Wait," cry the Smiths. "If we die together tomorrow, designated charities receive $8 million — $5 million more than each of our children." True. And if their assets (adjusted for inflation) rise beyond $20 million to $30 million or $40 million, the distribution will look like that in Table 13.

Comments on Prep Sheet Planning

So, thanks to the prep sheets, the Smiths can visualize what will transfer to whom, at whatever value their estate totals when they expire. Three points should be kept in mind when working with these prep sheets. First, asset sizes plotted should always stretch from virtually zero to the very maximum expected from a person's estate. In our example, ending the spreadsheets at $40 million is probably inadequate. There is nothing lost from listing significantly higher asset sizes. This may sound foolish, but stranger things have happened than the emergence of enormous, unforeseen values.

Consider the actual case of one family. The major asset of this family's wealth was a company, which at the time of the owner's death was thought to be worth around $10 million. Between the time that the owner died and when his legacies were distributed, the business was bought by a larger company for approximately forty times the $10 million. Yes, *forty* times. The owner's stock was sold, and the named individual and charitable-foundation beneficiaries suddenly were worth hundreds of millions. Whether the owner would have distributed such overwhelming amounts to individuals the way circumstances ultimately dictated is something we will never know. What we do know is that this question could have been avoided had the will

Table 12: Smith Inheritance Allotments ($13 million to $20 million in assets)
(Date: January 3, 1994. Table to be adjusted for U.S. Government C.P.I.)

| Combined Assets (in millions) | Inheritance Percentages Directed to | | | | Inheritance Dollars Received by | | | | Inheritance Taxes Paid | Total Received by Heirs and Charity |
| | Taxed Heirs | | Nontaxed Recipients | | Taxed Heirs[a] Cumulative Amounts (in millions) | | Nontaxed Recipients | | | |
	Child 1	Child 2	Charity A	Charity B	Child 1	Child 2	Charity A	Charity B		
$13	0%	0%	50%	50%	$3	$3	$0.5	$0.5	$6	$ 7
14	0	0	50	50	3	3	1.0	1.0	6	8
15	0	0	50	50	3	3	1.5	1.5	6	9
16	0	0	50	50	3	3	2.0	2.0	6	10
17	0	0	50	50	3	3	2.5	2.5	6	11
18	0	0	50	50	3	3	3.0	3.0	6	12
19	0	0	50	50	3	3	3.5	3.5	6	13
20	0	0	50	50	3	3	4.0	4.0	6	14

[a] Tax rate of 50%.

Table 13: Smith Inheritance Allotments ($30 million to $40 million in assets) (Date: January 4, 1994. Table to be adjusted for U.S. Government C.P.I.)

Combined Assets (in millions)	Inheritance Percentages Directed to					Inheritance Dollars Received by					Total
	Taxed Heirs		Nontaxed Recipients			Taxed Heirs[a]		Nontaxed Recipients		Inheritance Taxes	Received
						Cumulative Amounts (in millions)				Paid	by Heirs
	Child 1	Child 2	Charity A	Charity B		Child 1	Child 2	Charity A	Charity B		and Charity
$30	0%	0%	50%	50%		$3	$3	$ 9	$ 9	$6	$24
40	0	0	50	50		3	3	14	14	6	34

[a] Tax rate of 50%.

been written with built-in adjustments like the ones suggested
and with thoughts spelled out for varying allocations (if any) at
different estate levels.

Second, numerous combinations can be utilized in the prep
sheets — for example, not simply two children and two charities.
Include as many beneficiaries and different allocations as are appropriate to the situation. Elderly parents might be assured of
safety through a trust that lasts through their lifetime and reverts
upon their death to other heirs or designated charities.

Third and last, using prep sheets does not dismiss a person
from "checking in" with a financial adviser or lawyer, or from rethinking allocations as time goes on or circumstances change. In
any case, the prep sheet approach is dynamic and allows for easy
conversion to new conditions. And the ability to see precise numbers for the important factors constitutes a practical aid to better
decision making.

Chapter 23

The True Costs Associated with Charitable Giving, Plus the Delicate Challenge of When, if Ever, You Should Entertain Becoming a Serious Giver

BELIEVE it or not, there were times in US history when it was more cost-effective to give 100 percent of a given asset to charity than it was to sell the asset and retain the proceeds. Do not count on this recurring anytime soon. Unless the current tax laws change dramatically, there will always be a net cost to a donor, a cost that should be well understood in any contemplation of giving.

If a charitable gift consists of cash or of assets that would entail no capital gains tax if sold, the tax savings will always equal the existing ordinary tax rate; the net cost will always be the difference between the value given and this (federal and state ordinary income) tax rate. Give $100 when the ordinary tax rate is 33 percent and the savings will be $33; the net cost will be $100 minus $33, or $67.

Things get more complicated when the value of the gift is higher than its original cost. Savings and net costs then become dependent on (1) the relative cost basis of the donated asset and (2) applicable regulations concerning the respective tax rates on capital gains and ordinary income. The net-cost calculation is derived from comparing the return that would come from selling the asset outright (keeping the after-tax proceeds) with the tax benefits from donating it (only the tax savings are retained since the asset is now owned by the charity).

Table 14: True Cost of Gifting an Asset with Zero Cost Basis Versus Selling It

	1	2	3
	Asset Sold	Same Asset Given to Charity	Net Cost of Gift
Market value (proceeds from sale)	$100,000	(all to charity)	
Cost basis	0		
Capital gains tax due	(33,000)		
Tax reduction	0	$33,000	
Net benefit	$67,000[a]	$33,000[b]	$34,000[c]

[a] In after-tax retained assets.
[b] In cash from tax savings.
[c] The negative difference from giving versus selling.

Table 14 is a comparison of the outright sale of a zero original cost asset worth $100,000 and the gifting of that same asset. Figures are based on a combined state and federal income tax rate of 33 percent for both ordinary income and capital gains; it is assumed that the federal alternative minimum tax (AMT) does not apply.

The $100,000 asset sold would leave $67,000 after the capital gains tax. If it had been donated, a $33,000 tax deduction could be taken. Thus, in comparison with selling the $100,000 asset, donating it costs the giver only $34,000.

"But," you may be thinking, "the asset is gone. What's so attractive about retaining $34,000? Why not wait until I die and gift the same $100,000 to charity when inheritance tax laws allow 100 percent tax-free charitable giving?" There's more than one answer to this query, but the main one is that there is a "cost" incurred by waiting, too. This will be discussed at the end of this chapter.

Table 15 shows how net giving costs will vary with three considerations: original cost basis of the asset to be gifted, the capital gains tax rate, and the ordinary income tax rate.

Table 15: How Giving Costs Change, Depending on Cost Basis, Capital Gains, and Ordinary Income Tax Rates ($100,000 market value)

1	2	3	4	5
			Net Cost of Gift versus Sale, Assuming 23% Capital Gains Tax	
Cost Basis	Net Cost of Gift[a]	Net Cost of Gift as a Percentage[a,b]	Ordinary Tax Rate 33%	Ordinary Tax Rate 40%
0	$34,000[c]	34.00%	44.00%	37.00%
25%	42,250	42.25	49.75	42.75
50	50,500	50.50	55.50	48.50
75	58,750	58.75	61.25	54.25
100	67,000	67.00	67.00	60.00

[a] Assuming 33% tax rates for capital gains and ordinary income.
[b] Column 2 divided by $100,000.
[c] As per Table 14, column 3.

Table 15 Discussed

Columns 1, 2, and 3 reflect the same $100,000 fair-market-value gift and 33 percent tax rates for both ordinary income and capital gains as in Table 14. The exceptions here are the far right columns, where costs of a donor's giving versus selling use, first, in column 4, a lower, 23 percent capital-gains-tax assumption along with the same 33 percent ordinary income rate; and, second, in column 5, a 23 percent capital gains tax rate accompanied by a higher, 40 percent ordinary income tax.

As ordinary income tax rates rise, the net cost of donating obviously falls (and vice versa). Likewise, as capital gains tax rates decline, net donating costs of appreciated assets rise. To repeat, if donations are in cash or in assets with original cost identical to market value, the savings from gifts always equal the ordinary income tax rate.

One cautionary note: the percentages shown in columns 2 through 5 are obviously not additional to the effects that donating has on the givers' net worth, such as those presented earlier. The two tables here explain only the differences that exist as ordinary income and capital gains tax rates change, as well as when an individual contributes assets (with varying cost basis) versus selling them outright.

The Costs of Lost Opportunities

The elimination of an asset from net worth is not the only cost of giving. Obviously, the removal of compounding earning power from this net cost is a loss, too. Thus, even though a contributed dollar will lead to a tax deduction that lowers its expense below a dollar, the remainder is gone — as are its future earnings.

If you're a financial wizard such as George Soros, or Warren Buffett, with a record of earning huge annual returns on your money, every net dollar cost is expensive; after all, even 20 percent per year doubles your money in 3.8 years and then further compounds rapidly over time. It is easy, therefore, to rationalize nongiving by simply saying that charity is better off allowing you to compound these assets until they can be donated tax-free at death.

The counterarguments here are both humane and financial. For example, what are the expenses we incur by delaying cures for deadly diseases? Who can calculate the costs to individuals and to the nation of inadequate education available to a large majority of our school population for another full generation? Likewise, it is logical to assume that individuals capable of building fortunes possess exceptional creativity, energy, and managerial or entrepreneurial talents that could, if focused toward philanthropy, produce equally exceptional results. During World War II, countless people volunteered as "Dollar a Year" (their pay) executives, and many others have since given their time at financial sacrifices for a variety of government and nongovernment services. Still, money itself is essential. It should be a critical catalyst for constructive change. And as well-intended as an ultimate gift may be, either a delay in its availability or the pattern of its usage can be counterproductive in many ways. For example, consider the immensely wealthy Mr. X, whose assets and yearly income averaged between $500 million and $750 million and between $20 million and $40 million, respectively, over the past twenty years, but who has donated as little as a relatively paltry $250,000 to $1 million every year. In his sixties today, Mr. X has a life expectancy of perhaps another twenty years — and when he dies, whatever he leaves to charity will pass to a foundation that in turn will probably distribute only the required 5 percent of corpus to worthy causes. Mr. X may feel good about this, but you can see how much our society *and Mr. X* have missed already — and how little everyone will benefit compared to what would be derived if Mr. X adopted a plan of more generous current philanthropy and a more liberal donation policy after death. As the notable businessman and philanthropist Julius Rosenwald (of early Sears Roebuck fame) stated: "The millions that came to me at 50 could not restore a tooth I had lost at 30. They could not blot out a single day of grief." Furthermore, mental acuity often disintegrates long before death. When it does, the joys of giving are either reduced or never realized, and the probabilities of wise philanthropy are also diminished. So, the seemingly intangible costs of deferring philanthropic contributions to worthy causes for years, perhaps decades, can in fact be very substantial — and very disruptive — to individuals and society as a whole.

Shifting to positive examples, Mr. Soros started in 1984 to make substantial (over $1 billion) grants, some domestic and some pointed toward fostering open societies and freedom in Eastern Europe. And there are many more who are acting now, not waiting for the hereafter. But not enough — not enough recognizing that increased donations representing distinctly affordable portions of either income or corpus are small sacrifices when offset by the large potential benefits to themselves, to their family and community, and to society. Besides, how many of us can honestly say that our contributed dollars will cause us to miss out on dramatic investment returns? How many of us are George Soroses or Warren Buffets anyway?

Chapter 24

Plausible Spending or Giving Levels for More than 100 Different Income and Earning-Asset Combinations, with Estimated Wealth Results

I HOPE that enough reasoning and sufficient examples have been presented to persuade you that surplus money can be identified and possibly put to better use. Various levels of income and wealth have been discussed, but many more have been left out. So it is time to fill in some voids and present a table that covers numerous combinations of income and earning assets in order to help you decide what spending or giving *might* be prudent and to estimate what effect these suggestions *might* have on your future wealth.

It may seem unnecessary to repeat the warnings that have accompanied many of the recommendations made in this book, but certain caveats simply must reappear in this chapter. The *might* emphases in the first paragraph are there for good reason. In fact, they could have been accompanied by *possibly, perhaps,* and *maybe.* Let it be said again that the numbers and suggestions presented have been approached with conservatism, and with no implication that they represent exactness. All figures have to be considered as approximate, ballpark estimates. No one can predict accurately either the volatility or the outcomes of most income or net worth situations. Important ingredients such as the mix of investments owned, the rates of return they will generate, and the stability and liquidity of earning power or wealth are bound to be radically different from person to person. Furthermore, such personal factors as debts outstanding, insurance coverage, total expenses, housing fulfillment, health considerations, or family and other needs (including inheritance goals) — all of which influence financial decisions and eventual outcomes — can only be supplied by the person involved.

Allow me further to repeat that safety of principal is a prime consideration for almost all of us and that any capital withdrawal plan must be contingent on regular reassessments of your financial picture. Understanding that this kind of flexibility exists is critical to achieving financial peace of mind, and hence, to the adoption of most withdrawal plans.

This is not to negate the value of making projections and generalizations as I have in this book. The ability to recognize surplus money and to suggest how much of it, if any, might be used for chosen purposes — preferably philanthropy — is a positive exercise.

These warnings behind us, I can now proceed to suggest possible contribution levels and estimated inflation-adjusted wealth that *might* result over five-year and even longer periods. The matrix in Table 16 will allow you to

- match an approximate AGI with an EA amount;
- note an estimate of what might be an affordable charitable-donation figure for this AGI/EA combination; and
- learn from the same spreadsheet cell a guesstimated EA, adjusted for 3 percent inflation, that might exist at the end of five and ten years, given the evenly distributed annual financial assumptions explained in Chapter 15.

The Goals of the Matrix

There are countless ways to illustrate who might be able to afford given amounts of money. My decision was to set donation levels in Table 16 that allow the groups below $20 million EA to accumulate additional wealth, while those cells at or above $20 million EA were "allowed" only to retain their approximate asset values. All of the lower AGI/EA combinations end up with more real wealth than their base points. If any cells seem to produce inadequate estimated future EAs, it is generally because their earning assumptions are low (for example, an EA of $3.6 million with only $125,000 of AGI — only a 3 1/2% return including salaries, possible Social Security, and investment returns). It is usually this low return, and not the donation amount, that is responsible for any underachieving EA's in the table.

The decision to show the higher AGI/EA combinations retaining or slightly increasing their existing wealth is *not* to suggest that people with surplus money should preserve whatever they have. You know by now that most of the very wealthy can certainly afford some subtractions, and that I hope many people with well below $1.8 million in income and $16 million in EA will think it comfortable, wise, and even enjoyable to share at least some small portion of their riches. And you know furthermore that people with much lower EAs who have limited inheritance obligations or lower financial needs might consider some EA diminution, too. Hence, the donation levels are by no means meant to represent maximum numbers.

Table 16 Discussed

The matrix covers (in the top horizontal row) annual AGI levels ranging from zero on up to $100 million, while the vertical column lists EA ownership ranging from one hundred dollars to $500 million. All matrix numbers are stated in thousands of dollars.

If your interest is in the combination of an $85,000 AGI with a $150,000 EA, look for the "85" on the top row and "150" on the side column and then note within the table where these two categories converge. In this case, the first of the three numbers — the "3.7" — means that a $3,700 annual donation has been selected. The middle number "219" means that after five years an approximate $219,000 inflation-adjusted EA might result (versus the initial value of $150,000), assuming all the ratios presented in the book remain intact and are achieved in evenly distributed ways. The bottom number represents an estimated ten-year inflation-adjusted EA of $311,000 based on five years of advanced giving followed by a second five years of the actual 1991 giving ratios.

It would be virtually impossible to supply all income and EA levels, so I have included the 1991 average levels (highlighted in bold print), along with over 100 additional reference points. If broad conclusions suit you, simply glancing at various AGI/EA combinations will provide you with a sense of the donation suggestions and the possible wealth outcomes. There are, however, some general rules to observe in perusing this matrix, as follows:

1. There is a reasonable consistency in donation amounts *if you keep EA constant and look left or right across the numerous AGI levels.* If you choose a $150,000 EA, you can scan across the "150" row and note logical differences in donation levels as AGI changes from $35,500 all the way to $10 million. Do *not* expect *precise* progressions in any numbers presented, however, since living expenses, tax rates, and numerous other assumptions, may differ from level to level.

To determine information for an AGI amount that exists between two adjacent cells in the matrix, you can simply prorate for the numbers between the two closest AGIs. Hence, if you are interested in the $150,000 EA level with a $195,000 AGI, which is halfway between the "$125,000" and "$265,000" AGI columns, you can assume that approximately 50 percent of the differences between the "125" and "265" AGI cells on the "150" row qualifies as an appropriate donation level as well as the five- and ten-year wealth estimates. For example, the midpoint between the "7" and "19" donation suggestions is 13; and the estimated five-year EA is the midpoint between 278 and 443, or approximately 360 (thousand dollars).

2. The blank spaces in the matrix exist mainly where the EA and AGI seem out of proportion to one another. For example, the 1.2 percent return that a $590,000 income represents on a $50 million EA leaves little room for salary, dividends, or other earning sources built into the matrix program. Combinations such as these have been omitted because of the difficulties of adjusting the sources in reasonable ways and because doing so would create inconsistencies for this cell versus others.

3. There is a consistency in numbers when you glance diagonally at our matrix numbers, as per the seven 1991 average AGI/EA combinations used throughout the book (see the bold

Table 16: Suggested Possible Affordable Donation Levels Matrix, with Estimated Five- and Ten-Year Earning-Asset Results (adjusted for 3% inflation)

Annual Inc., AGI ($000)		35.5	60	85	125	265	590	1,000
Earning **$.1**	*Donation*	0.1	0.4	1.6	4.7	15	47	96
Assets	*EA Yr 5*	6	39	77	133	303	665	1,166
($000)	*EA Yr 10*	20	89	173	308	693	1,568	2,772
44		**0.5**	0.7	2.5	5.0	16	54	107
		49	82	117	177	346	688	1,170
		62	131	213	352	736	1,589	2,771
80		0.7	**1.5**	3.3	5.8	18	56	117
		85	**116**	150	211	377	719	1,175
		97	**164**	244	386	767	1,620	2,773
150		0.9	1.8	**3.7**	7.0	19	60	130
		155	186	**219**	278	443	777	1,213
		165	233	**311**	453	834	1,677	2,808
400		1.2	3.1	5.5	**9**	23	66	141
		407	438	466	**527**	689	1,015	1,437
		414	483	551	**703**	1,084	1,919	3,034
1,300			5.4	8.2	13	**33**	97	185
			1,340	1,376	1,447	**1,580**	1,844	2,223
			1,365	1,450	1,643	**1,987**	2,756	3,826
3,600					24	53	**121**	214
					3,755	3,897	**4,137**	4,510
					3,941	4,357	**5,093**	6,163
8,000						82	188	325
						8,294	8,473	8,716
						8,767	9,509	10,444
16,000							335	531
							16,227	16,376
							17,325	18,251
20,000							434	680
							20,000	20,000
							21,131	21,882
30,000								767
								30,000
								32,038
40,000								
50,000								
100,000								
250,000								
500,000								

(all values in thousands of dollars)

1,825	5,000	10,000	20,000	30,000	40,000	50,000	100,000
195	800	2,024					
2,311	6,703	13,374					
5,573	17,331	37,120					
206	803	2,033					
2,320	6,740	13,390					
5,579	17,368	37,131					
211	806	2,040					
2,341	6,766	13,402					
5,598	17,392	37,140					
217	818	2,056					
2,394	6,797	13,416					
5,650	17,419	37,145					
287	823	2,085	6,581				
2,426	7,040	13,574	19,000				
5,657	17,666	37,293	70,090				
352	995	2,215	6,767				
3,150	7,394	14,051	19,250				
6,375	17,949	37,712	70,231				
412	1,173	2,470	7,345	12,217			
5,340	9,190	15,562	19,500	19,800			
8,602	19,714	39,130	70,124	98,489			
602	1,688	3,397	8,581	13,799			
9,300	12,119	17,116	19,750	19,900			
12,599	22,497	40,261	69,645	97,796			
900	2,463	5,141	11,396	17,722			
16,672	18,102	19,813	19,900	20,000			
20,064	28,327	42,169	68,413	96,440			
1,132	3,031	6,282	13,261	20,591			
20,000	20,000	20,000	20,000	20,000			
23,386	29,967	41,749	67,829	95,702			
1,232	3,128	6,378	13,348	20,671	28,195		
30,000	30,000	30,000	30,000	30,000	30,000		
33,612	40,198	51,982	78,063	105,937	134,802		
1,321	3,226	6,474	13,437	20,748	28,265		
40,000	40,000	40,000	40,000	40,000	40,000		
43,750	50,429	62,214	88,297	116,172	145,037		
1,409	3,324	6,571	13,529	20,833	28,342	35,980	
50,000	50,000	50,000	50,000	50,000	50,000	50,000	
53,903	60,661	72,447	98,531	126,407	155,272	184,708	
	3,796	7,059	14,009	21,297	28,786	36,403	
	100,000	100,000	100,000	100,000	100,000	100,000	
	111,574	123,611	149,701	177,580	206,448	235,884	
		8,443	15,474	22,754	30,231	37,834	76,518
		250,000	250,000	250,000	250,000	250,000	250,000
		276,029	303,212	331,101	359,974	389,413	538,001
			17,748	25,170	32,674	40,273	78,936
			500,000	500,000	500,000	500,000	500,000
			556,662	586,356	615,851	645,295	793,875

print squares in the matrix). Diagonal cells such as these seven will show fairly consistent gradations and can be prorated for in-between points as per #1 above.

4.   There are some warnings to heed if you focus on a constant AGI and glance down the AGI column to changing EA levels. An unchanged AGI as EA grows forces higher absolute investment returns but offsets lower salary and other income to keep AGI the same, which in turn mutes relative donation potentials. Likewise, you should not assume that a jump in your EA will produce the same matrix results as a gradual evolution from your starting EA to the new level. To illustrate, if you start with a $1 million AGI and a $400 thousand EA and suddenly inherit $3.2 million, do not expect the 1,000/3,600 AGI/EA cell to represent your position. Your new AGI will soon be much higher than the original $1 million, so you need to estimate what your new income and EA will become before you can line up the proper matrix cell. (The horizontal and diagonal cells show consistency because the conditions and progressions affecting the individual cells are consistent, too). For detailed explanations of row, diagonal, and column data movements, see Appendix, pages 195–196.

5.   The bottom figure in every AGI/EA cell is the estimated EA after ten years on an inflation-adjusted basis.

6.   Once you have found the convergent AGI/EA zone of greatest interest to you, I recommend that you concentrate first on the five-year inflation-adjusted EA estimate (the middle number in that cell). If this figure appears comfortable, you might choose the stated donation number in the cell. If your personal EA five-year goal is higher than the EA cell shows, you should consider a lower donation number (or vice versa).

7.   You should compare your personal financial situation with the assumptions used in this book. Check your spending needs against the estimated expenses in Table 2 on page 51; and compare your investment diversification, rates of return, tax rate, and inflation assumptions with the figures on page 114.

8.   Most numbers have been rounded, both for ease of reading and to reiterate that no claims of statistical accuracy are made.

9.   The lowest 1991 bracket group shown in the matrix, with $35,500 AGI and $44,000 EA, shows a ("0.5") $500 donation

level that was the average number computed from the 1991 IRS statistics. As with other low-income, low-EA levels, it is hard to produce much growth in EA over time, but it is not the donation that precludes this.

10. Donation suggestions for most AGI/EA groups in Table 16 are well below the 10 percent (or higher) income tithes practiced by certain religious and other groups. The experience of the Mormon Church (The Church of Jesus Christ of Latter-day Saints) contradicts the matrix suggestions, as financial success of Mormons has resulted despite tithing principles substantially more stringent than the majority of contributions advanced here. Frugality, religious community support systems, and other factors, are obviously contributory factors to their success. In any case, the Mormon example lends further credence to the claim that my financial recommendations are conservative.

11. Table 16 also shows selective examples of donation levels higher than either tithing levels or 1994 IRS tax-deduction limits on contributions (the matrix adjusts for this and omits deductions for anything exceeding 50 percent of AGI). As discussed, these were allowed for illustrative purposes only — to show how much might be donated and still allow existing asset ownership to persist. Remember, too, that an initial strategy of five years or less of advanced donations has been suggested throughout this book, and that EA estimates of ten years and beyond that produce higher wealth figures occur after a return to old giving habits.

12. While my tax rate assumptions are generally higher than might exist for the average taxpayer, concentration has been on federal levies. Because they are so varied, no attempt was made to incorporate state income taxes, but (because both are deductible) you can adjust donations downward for the state levies with no effect on forecasted five- and ten-year EAs. The only time this is not true is if donations exceed 50 percent of AGI and then lose their write-off possibilities.

If philanthropy is not your goal, you can substitute incremental personal spending for any part of the donation number in your matrix cell. You should, however, reduce the estimated wealth numbers by the amount of any lost tax savings resulting from the substitution. For example, if the donation number within the AGI/

EA cell of your choice is $3,000 and your tax bracket is approximately 33 percent, the $1,000 per year tax deduction that no longer applies (times five, for the five-year period used in the matrix) will lower the ultimate EA by approximately $5,000. It is up to you to decide whether the $5,000 reduction leaves you with sufficient EA protection.

To conclude, you should now possess a broader understanding of affordability potentials. You will want to double-check the many personal and financial factors mentioned before you take any actions, but you should be better prepared to make more intelligent decisions about money and its potential uses — particularly the productive investment that philanthropy should, and can, be.

Chapter 25

How Much Healing of America Might Be Accomplished? And How the Government Might Provide Greater Incentives to Private-Sector Contributors

LET'S look now at the potential impact of increased giving and see what we can hope to achieve. Table 17 is a "scoreboard" showing the one-year possibilities that exist from the various groups and subgroups discussed.

Table 17 Discussed

As column 6 shows, the total one-year increase from this series of conservative suggestions amounts to a staggering $102 billion. Impressive as these figures are, they represent only the combination of the top five individual tax-filing brackets and the select group of foundations and corporations. Untouched are the two AGI individual filing brackets (covering $25,000 to $75,000) that in 1991 accounted for slightly more contributions in absolute dollars than the groups shown in Table 17, column 4, combined. And the corporations sampled obviously represent but a fraction of US businesses, just as the cited foundations represent only a portion of the nonprofits. Likewise, since these statistics were based on 1991 figures, an upward adjustment for inflation and a stronger economy might be appropriate. So you can see the potentials. Indeed, it's this sort of incremental money that can initiate the conversion of a struggling society to a healthy one.

Table 17: Increased Giving Potential from Individuals and Institutions Using the Reaching Out Model

	1	2	3	4	5	6
	1991 Average Contribution (in thousands)	Potential Affordable Donation Using Reaching Out Model (in thousands)	Increase Suggested by Reaching Out Model[a]	Actual Giving in 1991 (in billions)	Absolute Giving Levels Suggested by Reaching Out Model (in billions)	Increase in Giving Using Reaching Out Model (in billions)
Individuals in 1991— average AGI (in thousands)						
$1,825	$87	$900	10.3 times	$4.5	$46.3	$41.8
590	18	121	6.7	2.2	14.7	12.5
265	7	33	4.7	5.0	23.5	18.5
125	3	9	3.0	8.3	24.9	16.6
85	2	4	2.0	7.1	14.2	7.1
Subtotal				27.1	123.6	96.5
Foundations in 1992			1.3 times	9.2	12.0	2.8
Corporations in 1991 (304 corporations)			2.5 times	1.9	4.7	2.8
TOTAL				38.2	140.3	102.1

[a] Expressed as a multiple of the 1991 average contribution.

And the Effects of Higher Deductions on Government Deficits?

As discussed, one proverbial "fly in the ointment" from greater charitable giving is the effect that increased tax deductions would have on federal and state governmental deficits. Assuming an average 33 percent tax rate, the government deficits would swell by $30 billion to $35 billion in the first year of such giving — not a pretty picture — although there are dynamic prospects from an incremental $100 billion suddenly going to fine causes. Of course, the hope is that well-focused private giving could relieve local, state, and federal agencies from their spending needs — possibly well beyond the tax deduction totals.

To avoid immediate enlarged deficits, though, givers ought to pinpoint and direct a meaningful portion of their donations to specific current programs. This is not to suggest that established nonprofit endowments and capital programs should be neglected. Givers will probably wish to carry on with what they have been doing in terms of supporting nonprofits. Efficient nonprofit organizations, large and endowed though they may be, may tackle new challenges better than many start-ups or smaller, possibly less effective entities. To give only to endowments, however, particularly to those likely to allocate just a very small percentage toward specific current projects, will not do the trick. As mentioned, only about 5 percent of a donation to an endowment will, on average, have an impact, and only after earning its first year's interest. Hence, even enhanced giving for new programs within organizations that persist with their normal absolute spending will not supply the desired impetus. Still, the thesis is sound: Solutions to enough problems, along with increased public insistence on less government involvement, is a strong combination to produce lower deficits.

Structural Changes Are Needed

There are, of course, important legal and structural changes in the tax codes that could be enacted to complement and even encourage the strategies described in this book. Here are some thoughts in that regard — some practical, some "pie in the sky," but all worth at least a modicum of consideration.

• *Why not* reduce certain restrictions on the gifting of appreciated (that is, low-cost) holdings to charities?* The 1993 tax changes took a step in this direction by eliminating the "alternative minimum tax penalties," but larger and more immediate donations would be encouraged by raising the deductibility percentage of AGI allowed for low-cost contributions.

• *Why not* consider Peter Drucker's challenge to allow "taxpayers to deduct $1.10 for each dollar they give to nonprofits as a cash donation"?

• *Why not* alter other deductibility rules to encourage higher levels of donations? Tax authorities cannot factor in net worth, but they might introduce a graduated, sliding scale of tax deductions, perhaps based on percentage of income donated — with smaller write-offs for the smaller (relative to income) givers and larger deductions for the larger givers. In order to pass the "revenue-neutral" test that accompanies most tax change proposals today, more demanding gifts might be required of high-bracket filers in order for them to receive deductions comparable to low-bracket givers.

• *Why not* provide special incentives for contributions to nonprofits set up to spend their capital over maximum periods of time (for example, higher deductions for funds that are fully expended within one, five, or ten years)?

• *Why not* create incentives for people to start earlier in their lives with major donations? IRS actuarial tables that determine tax deductibility for contributions to various charitable trusts might be liberalized. Incentives to donate earlier could bolster the "preventive medicine" that our society needs. If instituted, however, they would no doubt require special regulations.

• *Why not* allow special deductions for contributing to areas identified by the government as "critical," perhaps with the proviso

---

*Taxpayer deductions are currently limited to 20 percent of AGI for donations to related family foundations and 30 percent for gifts to independent charities if contributions consist of appreciated holdings, versus a 50-percent-of-AGI deduction limit for cash or non-capital-gains asset donations.

that private-sector contributions substitute for certain anticipated governmental expenditures. Hence, the deductions that reduce tax receipts might pale in comparison to private investments in "controlled" areas. Needless to say, this would require considerable organization and sharp controls, as well as a stipulation that dollars be placed in use immediately for incremental program spending rather than be "warehoused" by the recipient organizations.

• *Why not* simply allow special giving deductions for funds put to immediate use versus those warehoused? Care would have to be taken not to discourage gifts to endowments and comparable worthwhile pools used to support capital improvements or other essential "rainy day" needs. But perhaps reducing tax deductions for donations to nonprofits that spend exceedingly low amounts of their capital could encourage a better balance between immediate-use funds and those to be used in the distant future.

• *Why not* tighten charitable-deduction allowances for gifts of cash and personal possessions in order to make sure that giving occurs and that it is worthy of deductibility?

• *Why not* also tighten standards for nonprofit status, so as to eliminate abuses and divert potentially "wasted" tax revenues to true philanthropic efforts?

• *Why not* allow for special deductions to joint private/public programs such as the government's Head Start or America 2000 efforts?

• *Why not* urge states that levy their own separate income taxes to create imaginative financial incentives to alleviate isolated regional needs?

• *Why not* add to the current rule that requires foundation grants to average 5 percent of corpus. A formula that adjusts for negative investment experience, yet forces a sharing of inflation-adjusted investment gains that exceed a certain level, might produce a more equitable system. The goal would be to encourage funds that grow dramatically in size to share more of their largesse for the very purposes of their existence.

No doubt there are many other possible incentives to stimulate more generous giving by those who can afford it. Given the po-

tential positives, a constructive new look at our system seems
warranted. Difficult problems often require innovative, even controversial, solutions. Consider how monetary policies in the late
1980s and early 1990s bolstered profitability of US commercial
banks and converted an ailing system to a healthy one. Think how
the reduction of income taxes from write-offs encouraged American businesses to take harsh measures that ultimately led to lower
costs and greater competitiveness. These and other incentives
should eventually lead to sharply higher tax receipts for our country. It's about time that politicians and legislators alter their views
that charitable deductions constitute, at best, a "tax loophole."
Quite the contrary: enlightened giving can be among the most efficient, productive remedies for the huge problems that plague us.

Chapter 26

How Private Citizens Can Triumph over Public Obstacles

IN THE 1830s the astute French political observer Alexis de Tocqueville marveled at the propensity of Americans to form "intellectual and moral associations," especially those that went beyond politics and commerce. Our country's history is filled with successful examples of community, civic, and other associations that have solved problems and enhanced the quality of our lives. Volunteer projects that are sensitive to the needs of others are what impressed Tocqueville most, and fortunately many are in existence today. But a great opportunity exists to improve, and in some cases expand, these organizations. This is the most efficient route to overcoming the burgeoning obstacles facing individuals, communities, and our nation as a whole.

Failure to resolve many of our most severe problems often stems from the inability of individuals, businesses, nonprofits, and governments to shoulder the financial burdens of the cures. But financial strains are not the only reason for failure. Sadly, too many of our procedures have proved slow and ineffective. As a consequence, too many of our citizens have either lost faith in our system or have adopted attitudes that favor their narrow interests to the detriment of their neighbors or their country. Disenchantment with our system is more pervasive now than it has been in many decades.

Nevertheless, the United States still has a huge core of solid citizens who, given a glimmer of hope, will vote and act for a return of our unique American values. They will even make personal sacrifices to produce an improved environment for their communities. As a matter of fact, countless new and innovative efforts are surfacing in all parts of our nation.

But the workers and the leaders need encouragement. They need to know that funds will be available. And they need a plan attractive enough to create new civic-minded associations or to add new dimensions to existing ones, with special focus on local and regional causes. Money, time, and effort will be more forthcoming from people who can envision effective solutions to their local problems, and more dramatic impacts (more "punch" per investment dollar) can normally be realized on smaller, regional needs than on huge, national causes.

Fortunately, some fine examples are being set. There is The Atlanta Project (TAP), a vision of former president Jimmy Carter to improve the quality of life in a section of this Georgia city long riddled with crime, homelessness, poverty, drug abuse, and health deficiencies. TAP is combining its leadership and resources with private volunteer and community involvement. Its goal is to rehabilitate a disgraceful ghetto environment and ultimately turn it over to its inhabitants, who could never dream of such prospects without TAP.

Then there is Chicago's MacArthur Foundation, the country's sixth wealthiest, which is following a different but equally encouraging tack. MacArthur is increasing its support of neighborhood groups throughout the country, planting the seeds for the fertile combination of philanthropy and interested residents. Dynamic local leadership is the key to this success. So let me show you some illustrations of how local people can manage a transition to constructive change.

It may sound less action-oriented, but one thing donors can do to elevate the role of community service, encourage high ethics, and foster unusual contributions to the community is to establish more award programs. The wealthy will always rate media attention, but the accolades should be concentrated more on good deeds and meaningful monetary *sharing* as opposed to accumulation and luxurious living. Proper publicity, and in some cases financial rewards, should focus instead on the people and associations that are making positive things occur. Recognition such as the Pierre de Coubertin International Fair Play Trophy (named for founder of the modern Olympic Games), which has been awarded to athletes annually since 1964, is one model. Winners of this honor receive rave publicity for their sportsmanship, not their athletic acumen. Exceptional citizenship, leadership, and efforts on behalf of worthy causes should be recognized in the same manner.

Enthusiasm, involvement, volunteerism, sound management, and supportive money constitute the central tenets of Reaching Out. Where necessary, the willingness to fight for constructive change is essential, too. Let me describe, for instance, specific efforts that are improving education in given communities.

Let's start with the need for more and better schools in many regions of America. New York City was one area with clear needs for new schools, and the Aaron Diamond Foundation (uniquely created to give all of its money away within ten years) set out to help remedy this. Working with an established nonprofit, the Fund for New York City Public Education ("the Fund"), the Diamond group was joined by other foundations to develop numerous small, theme-driven, community-supported schools focused on adolescents. Within two years, sixteen New Vision High Schools were born, and another thirty or more similar schools are in sight. But it wasn't easy getting there. Obstacles, roadblocks, and delays were widespread, but the external coalition of philanthropists and the Fund remained diligent and have achieved significant progress. A passive, "we'll-give-you-money-with-no-strings-attached" approach would probably have failed.

Preschool, an essential need, is another example. Educators and sociologists will tell you that in many cases waiting for socially deprived children to enter kindergarten is simply too late. Too often bad habits have already been formed, and self-image has already become battered. Creating proper school environments early and involving parents more are ways to offset difficult home conditions. Local involvement can be especially effective here. Preschools can be formed independently, without external interference, since they are not official responsibilities of most public school districts. Or government programs can be upgraded — as they have been by philanthropists at the Honeywell Corporation, who wanted to catch kids before they fell into hopeless situations but who found government programs in Minneapolis to be inefficient and cumbersome. A "Success By Six" (SBS) plan developed new systems that tied together education, health, and welfare programs to help children prepare for schooling. SBS in effect redefined relationships between various government agencies and eventually implemented greatly enhanced services. Without the private-sector bankrolling and managerial leadership, the government structural problems would have persisted, and the futures of many thousands of young lives would have remained hopeless.

Shifting to later school levels, it is essential to attract and then retain the best teachers, and to see that they receive continuous retraining. Chicago businessperson Martin Koldyke did exactly this, by providing university scholarships to extraordinary teachers and by paying for the college education of students willing to commit themselves to teaching in the Chicago public schools. Programs modeled around Koldyke's plan should be promoted to a series of communities. The obstacles would be few and the rewards many.

Another example of strengthening teaching methods brought unusual pleasure to my wife and me. As in so many communities, San Francisco teachers often lack the time to share thoughts about the burdens that confront them daily (including noncurriculum difficulties such as language and cultural differences, drug and sex education, and other concerns). By sponsoring a one-week "Leadership and Development" retreat in a quiet, pleasant setting seventy-five miles south of the city, we brought together 110 teachers, administrators, and parents representing thirty-one schools. Objectives centered on learning common techniques to solve everything from one school's unsuccessful science curriculum to another's diverse ethnic/cultural problems and another's need for conflict resolution. In addition to their professional development, the teachers — who ought to be told every day how much they are needed — felt appreciated and returned to their schools with enthusiasm and fresh ideas.

Another example: Many school districts in our country are overstaffed with supervisors and understaffed on the teacher firing line. Here is where the private sector might accomplish what the politicians will not touch — by offering a variety of perks, including executives loaned by the business community to implement greater administrative efficiencies and help school systems adopt a more productive mix of teachers and supervisors. Trading philanthropic capital or managerial expertise for changes in an inefficient system is one unfortunate but necessary path to many accomplishments.

There are countless ways for the private sector to achieve critical changes and soon turn communities, and then our nation, around. But we need formal plans, and I suggest two specific ideas. The first is a coalition of wealthy local citizens who combine to attack the most serious three or four problems in their region. A handful of high-wealth, committed individuals might form a nucleus that commits to a new three- to five-year financial plan to concentrate on the agreed-upon maladies. The group should agree that the committed money will supplement (not supplant) what they are already contributing. They should be clear in their intent to force changes where necessary: to leverage what will become major funds to bring about changes quickly. They will probably want to attract perhaps ten to thirty additional financial partners, who agree that management responsibility will be concentrated through a small executive committee that is supported by a tight and knowledgeable paid staff. The staff and leadership people alike must listen to the people who are closest to the issues and most likely to be affected by proposed solutions.

While this all sounds like just another community fund or private foundation, the differences will be a highly focused concentration on no more than a handful of problems, grantmaking pinpointed to a small geographic region, a willingness to negotiate strenuously for systemic changes, and the utilization of the bulk of the money over a limited time period. In short, making a difference *now*, when it's so desperately needed.

The second idea is the formation of a national advisory board as an extension of the local coalitions just described. Its mission would be to help these private-sector "start-ups" by sharing with them the failures and successes experienced by its members. This advisory body might also seem like a duplication of existing

systems. The Foundation Center, numerous regional grantmaking bodies, the Social Venture Network, Business for Social Responsibility, the National Civic League's "American Renewal
Project," and working groups on philanthropy that include
countless law firms, investment organizations, banks, and other
entities of all sorts already exist, as do think tanks like the Manhattan Institute for Policy Research — all are offering provocative thoughts on ways to deal with municipal deficiencies
and other social problems. The major difference of my suggested advisory board would be the limited focus. The organization would only serve constituents whose interests centered on a
handful of problems. It would be a high-tech communication
center focusing cooperation and information sharing for its participants.

But we need to take these ideas even further, and we need a
clear, specific vision of our goals and needs. Here is a guideline to
get us from our current negatives to future positives.

Guideline for a Reaching Out Coalition

1. As stressed, local programs should be emphasized. Contributors should unite into coalitions willing to concentrate on the
most pressing regional needs. It should be agreed that cooperation
with local governments and existing entities is favored, but that
bold measures will be encouraged where necessary to overcome
obstacles.

2. As also described, a tight, centralized national leadership
should be formed — probably a board of directors of no more than
seven knowledgeable individuals, supported by a staff of less than
a dozen. The national board should concentrate on the successes
and failures of the regional parts and efficiently communicate with
"member" coalitions about their experiences. The national group's
recommendations should not be mandatory, however, lest the system become too bureaucratized.

3. Local groups should embark on three- to five-year plans.
As with personal Reaching Out, attitudes are likely to be more
positive if contributors can plan their giving over a period that is
long enough to allow a tax-efficient spreading of their donations,

yet short enough that the effects will be enjoyed by the contributors. Spacing out donations also removes the likelihood that government tax receipts will experience severe shortfalls, resulting in larger deficits.

4. As with American industry's broader search for world competitiveness, obstructive forces within the human-services industry must recognize the urgency for solutions. Entrenched and inefficient entities (possibly governments and nonprofits alike) must take their clues from what has occurred (and is still occurring) in so many US industries. Human-services providers must acknowledge what enlightened labor unions and company managements have recognized: the urgency to produce greater output and improved customer satisfaction lest they cede their existence to competitors. For example, public education will either have to become more effective or private schools, with or without voucher legislation, will prevail. In this case, enlightened philanthropy should demand that obstacles and excessive costs of certain public school systems be eliminated in exchange for certain private-sector donations.

5. We need mergers and consolidations of existing private programs. Personal agendas, egos, and historical traditions must give way to shared resources. In many instances, private- and public-sector cooperation will work best. The idea is to create a "me and thee" team, not a "them and us." Efforts such as the Head Start and America 2000 programs (public/private attempts to overcome the US education shortfalls) might, properly funded, unleash great force toward attacking numerous problems crying for solution. While government will continue to be the leader in countless areas, the merging of existing programs with private efforts might prove appropriate. In many cases, overall responsibility, modern methods, and authority will best reside with private-sector management.

6. Causes must be isolated and limited. Treating all the problems is impossible and is certain to drain resources. Concentration on priorities such as education, job training, and reduced crime may be all that can be handled efficiently at the beginning by these local entities.

7. Programs should consider inducing young people and other

targeted groups to serve by offering them payment in the form of vocational training, eventual school tuition, and the like. Businesses and professional schools of all sorts should emphasize the importance of community service and volunteerism. As Harvard Medical School psychologist Steven Berglas says, "Take your next class of MBAs and sentence them. Insist that they be a part of a community."

8. Leadership should draw from vibrant, talented managers who are willing to work for small remuneration. A "Peace Corps" of successful executives to work on domestic solutions should be developed at both the regional and the advisory board levels.

9. Pork barrel and special-interest demands must be avoided. Decisions must be based on goals that benefit broad groups, not on narrow requests that favor private interests that interfere with progress for the community.

10. Plans must not be allowed to disintegrate after the initial investment period. If all goes well, new financial and working participants will join and ultimately succeed the original groups; but even without this happening, sufficient maintenance of successful programs must be planned for beyond the official period. In other words, the organizations should operate as good businesses do, with near- and long-term planning involved.

11. Legislation should be encouraged to improve the prospects for the plan's success. Financial incentives may be needed. For example, greater flexibility might be created for donations earmarked for specific problems. Some of Chapter 25's suggestions to allow larger donations without penalties or to encourage greater gifting while living (after all, charitable gifts at death produce zero dollars to the government) should be devised — for, say, the three-to-five- and up-to-ten-year periods in which capital is fully expended.

12. As private-sector monies treat the systemic problems, governments must agree to cut their spending by the same or preferably larger dollar amounts. They need not do so in the same areas that are receiving aid; in fact, it might be best to use master cost-cutting lists such as the Grace Report or the more recent recommendations of the Concord Coalition, the budget cutting in favor of private-sector innovation and productivity as specified by the Progressive Policy Institute, the "A to Z Spending Cuts Plan"

sponsored by Representatives Andrews (D., N.J.) and Zeliff (R., N.H.) — or, of course, comparable wish lists from local sources.

13. It is important for all participants to recognize the unfortunate need for lobbying and political posturing in the United States today. It is true that those with the strongest needs (like the young) often have the weakest advocacy. One would like to think that a plan such as this would have few opponents, but contributors should be prepared to do what is necessary to build support. Ideally, any sums directed toward political efforts to effect change will be tiny compared to expenditures for specific, needy causes, but sensitivity to the political process is a fact of life.

This outline is not presented as a final, polished programmatic guide. It is offered as another impetus toward the proper investment in our country's future that is so critically needed. We should look for other plans and more ideas. For example, the Strategic Plan of President Carter's Atlanta Project contains similar tenets, plus many more specifics. Ideally, TAP will succeed and then serve as a more detailed, proven blueprint for other communities for at least certain aspects of its plan. After all, it combines Reaching Out's local involvement with what could become an efficient national observer — a central station to avoid reinventing the wheel everywhere, an active analyst of existing programs and procedures, and a communicator to those looking for guidance. Combining this new private-sector "army" with the basics covered in this text is certainly an improved way to convert the many negatives of our society to significant positives. But there can be no delay: we can no longer deprive today's children, and we should not allow another generation to come of age in the shadow of today's troubles.

Chapter 27

When Thomas Jefferson, Andrew Carnegie, John Gardner, and Jimmy Carter Meet

MILLIONS of individuals have served as great role models throughout our country's history. Some were ordinary folks who went out of their way to help others. Some were great leaders: philosophers, teachers, professional and business people, military and religious persons — and, yes, even politicians. Four people have been especially important to me in formulating the thesis for this book.

The first was Thomas Jefferson. I can picture his puzzlement over the current condition of the system he helped found, wondering how we will survive with a populace voting less and less, and when it does vote, supporting candidates and causes more out of personal interests than for the good of the whole. And I can almost hear his voice saying (as he did)

> I deem it the duty of every man to devote a certain portion of his income for charitable purposes . . . to do the most good of which he is capable . . . best insured by keeping within the circle of his own inquiry and information the subjects of distress to whose relief his contributions should be applied.

And I can certainly picture Jefferson pushing for nonprofits to elevate us from our weakened position. If the figure of ninety million or more Americans currently serving as volunteers is correct, Jefferson would probably have been encouraged. These numbers might have pointed him to the solutions emphasized in the preceding pages: to the huge pool of capital available for eleemosynary purposes; to the potential from combining an army of volunteers with increased funds; and to the importance of a better developed, Reaching Out nonprofit effort, with cooperation among the many sectors of our nation crying for constructive change.

A second model was Andrew Carnegie, businessman turned philanthropist who wrote *The Gospel of Wealth* over a century ago. Carnegie eloquently made the case that leadership by the wealthy would bring about constructive changes in society. While a believer in free competition, which he pragmatically assumed would inevitably concentrate wealth into "the hands of the few," Carnegie also firmly contended that the wealthy had a definite responsibility to redistribute excesses.

Carnegie said that "an ideal State [is one] in which the surplus wealth of the few will become . . . the property of many . . . administered for the common good." "The public verdict," he said, "will then be: 'The man who dies . . . rich dies disgraced.' " My guess is that Carnegie would be extremely upset over today's giving habits. He would have jumped at the chance to analyze and utilize the kind of data now available. Carnegie, like Jefferson, lived when communications were archaic compared to today, and when data presented inadequate information about income and a corresponding inability to estimate net worth or, of course, charitable generosity. In fact, Carnegie would no doubt have argued for considerably more generous donation levels — perhaps much higher than have been suggested here.

Carnegie also understood that money is only fuel to enable the engine to run better. Volunteers are absolutely crucial to addressing most needs, and every effort should be made to harness the very good people who are willing to devote time and energy to help needy causes. The marriage of money and volunteerism can create a spirit, a civic pride, that just might move mountains.

Third, I turn again to John Gardner, a model of leadership, who gives us this informed, articulate perspective.

Today our communities need us, desperately need our loyalty, our understanding, our support. . . . This nation is facing a test of character, all the more profound for being diffuse, all the more difficult for not being precipitated by enemy attack. The test is whether in all the confusion and clash of interest, all the distracting conflicts and cross purposes, all the temptations to self-indulgence and self-exoneration, we have the strength of purpose, the guts, the conviction, the spiritual staying power to build a future worthy of our past. You can help.

Gardner is obviously suggesting that the "help" must come from our citizenry — from those of us who, by Reaching Out, can afford to give the time, leadership, and money to the critical causes. In fact, Reaching Out mirrors the very individualism that made America great. It also provides the ideal channel for the required energy for change, as it provides a speedier process than other approaches. It is a movement to get individuals and the private sector more in charge of their own destinies, with less reliance on the many public institutions that have reduced our confidence in the future.

And last, Jimmy Carter is backing his words about breaking the poverty cycle, linking neighborhood values with national goals, and providing opportunity for the disadvantaged through his Atlanta Project and other Carter Center activities. Carter is serving as a model leader of movements that are encouraged by this book. An influential spokesman for the conscience of this country, if but an iota of his convictions and his willingness to fight for change could rub off on to more of us, the United States would benefit enormously.

Integral to this is the emphasis on *family*, whether it be blood relatives, neighbors, or those who constitute broad communities that surround us. As with family values, Reaching Out encourages attributes that will strengthen our youth, reinstate the concept of cooperation for the good of the whole, and enhance both individual and community pride and self-esteem. Furthermore, it in no way deprives anybody of the right to accumulate wealth. Quite the contrary, as suggested in my discussion of Trickle Down economics, more generous Reaching Out in the 1980s could have solved enough of today's problems that politicians would have had less need to consider hiking taxes. Perhaps they would have stronger faith in the stimulative effects of lower taxes. Hence, Reaching Out utilizes free enterprise to achieve better solutions to our nation's problems while it adds special meaning to the lives of both the contributors and the recipients. It provides the path for the providers to get more out of their existence, while naturally enhancing the lives of those less fortunate. It is a repeat of the successes of ancient Greece, which encouraged wealthy citizens to donate money and then carry out the activities that created the public improvement. In our case, the combination of charitable contributions and Reaching Out leadership can undo systemic problems and place America on the path to massive improvement. It is the personification of Jefferson, Carnegie, John Gardner, Alexander Hamilton, Benjamin Franklin, Jimmy Carter, and countless others.

The fact is that many of those who believe that they "simply can't afford" higher giving really can. And these potential healers of America's wounds are everywhere. A grand dream would be that many more of us recognize this and learn to derive greater pleasure from our collective, expanded efforts. Giving should be a joy, as I have shown with true-to-life examples throughout this book. Even in literature, one of the happiest endings occurs in Charles Dickens's *A Christmas Carol*. Ironically, Ebenezer Scrooge is generally remembered as a villain, depriving others and even himself; yet the enlightenment he ultimately experienced from sharing is undoubtedly the moral that Dickens intended. This sense of satisfaction is especially important, since people constantly struggle to find contentment in their lives, and also because fulfillment can become even more elusive as we grow older. Since none of us is growing younger, we should consider the outlets such as effective philanthropy that offer the opportunity to make us feel more productive.

The truth is, we cannot afford *not* to make the relatively small, intelligent financial commitments that are so affordable — commitments capable of generating significant positive changes for our society. We simply have to conduct a "war" on our problems, a war in which we are saving, not risking, lives. A specified, finite period of enhanced giving could help to produce a movement seldom duplicated in the history of the United States. It could usher in an era of elevated human spirit, a renaissance that could reverse many of the problems that have weakened our great nation.

Despite our country's problems, the vast majority of us should hold our heads high and count our blessings as Americans. We still represent a nation of opportunity, a people from diverse backgrounds integrated into a common bond of providing life, liberty, and the pursuit of happiness, along with a caring for the goodwill of human beings everywhere. To have faltered as we have is not abnormal. To recover is in our power.

In that spirit, the future and our fate are in our own hands. We have an obligation to Reach Out to help others, and those who can afford it must lead the way. Now is the time to impose a small voluntary "tax" on ourselves — or better stated, now is the time to invest wisely, to invest in something that is bound to end up being for ourselves, our loved ones, as well as for so many others who deserve an improved environment and whose elevation will strengthen our nation's present and future. Yes, the relative "decline and fall of the American empire" can be reversed. The world champion country can be saved, and you, your family, your community, and our populace can be happier and more fulfilled than ever.

Appendix

Note: All dollar numbers in the Appendix represent thousands — hence, as with the Table 16 matrix itself, three zeroes should be added to all dollar figures.

Following are three examples to explain movement of numbers in the Table 16 matrix presented on pages 170–171. These examples start with AGI = $1,000 and EA = $400,000, implying a recommended donation of $141. (Assume that overall income yield from EA is approximately 6%.):

    1. *Horizontal movement along the 400 EA row:* Assume AGI suddenly increases to 1,825, an advance of 825. Since EA is the same in a row, there is no change in initial investment yields and all the 825 increase is assumed to represent an increase in wages and salary. So, the sudden increase in AGI was a promotion or new job, that is, movement along a row means a change in initial salary.
Before: 400EA × 6% = 24. Therefore, Salary (= 1,000 − 24) = 976. Matrix data: Donation = 141; estimated 5-year EA = 1,437.
After: 400EA × 6% = 24, as previously. Therefore, Salary is now 1,825 − 24 = 1,801. New (1,825/400 AGI/EA) matrix data: Donation = 287; estimated 5-year EA = 2,426.
    The model has escalated living expenses and taxes appropriate to the new AGI = 1,825 level. Unspent balance flows into increased EA in year 2. Salary will grow at 3%; the new EA will grow at about 6%. The matrix shows the giving ability before (141) and after (287) the sudden increase in initial salary.
    2. *Vertical movement down the 1,000 AGI column:* Assume EA suddenly increases to 3,600, an increase of 3,200. Since AGI is the same in a column, the returns to the increased EA must therefore be exactly offset by lowered wages and salary: Initially, AGI was composed of the following:
Before: 400EA × 6% = 24. Therefore, Salary (= 1,000 − 24) = 976. Matrix data: Donation = 141; estimated 5-year EA = 1,437.

After: 3,600EA × 6% = 216. Therefore, Salary (= 1,000 − 216) = 784, a decline of 976 − 784 = 192, exactly equal to the increased yield (3,200 EA × 6% = 192) from EA. New matrix data: Donation = 214; Estimated 5-year EA = 4,510.

Hence, staying in the column means that the sudden increase of EA by 3,200 is accompanied by a demotion, new job, or reduced salary paying 192 ($192,000) less per year. Not a common situation. As a result, capacity for giving does not increase as dramatically going down a column because increased yields from the new EA are offset in year 1 by lowered initial salary to keep initial AGI = 1,000. The reason donations go up at all is due to the faster assumed real growth in EA than in salary in future years, leading to net increased giving capacity in future years.

3. *Diagonal movements*: Assume an inheritance of earning assets causes EA to advance suddenly to 3,600, an increase of 3,200, with AGI rising along with the EA. Salary stays the same (no new job or promotion). Therefore, EA and AGI *both* go up initially.
Before: 400EA × 6% = 24. Therefore, Salary (= 1,000 − 24) = 976. Matrix data: Donation = 141; estimated 5-year EA = 1,437.
After: 3,600EA × 6% = 216. Salary is unchanged at 976. Therefore, new initial AGI = 216 + 976 = 1,192. The new point, EA = 3,600 and AGI = 1,192 is not given on the matrix. So 1,192 is the AGI number you are attempting to assess in the new and enlarged (3,600 EA) row. Since 1,192 is between the 1,000 and 1,825 AGI columns, you should key off of the lower figure, or 1,000. Assuming that you are seeking the donation level, note the 214 in the 1,000/3,600 AGI/EA cell. Then, determine first the difference in AGI (1,192−1,000 = 192) you are attempting to resolve. Next, note the difference in donation levels in the 3,600 row between the 1,000 and 1,825 AGI columns: 412−214 = 198, which should be divided by the AGI column difference of 1,825−1,000 = 825. Since 198/825 = 0.24, you should now multiply 0.24 times the 192 AGI difference. This equals 46, which should be added to the 214 base, for a total of 260. So the new recommended donation is 260. Interpolation may also be used to arrive at the new estimated 5- and 10-year EAs. Factoring now for the 5-year EA, follow the same procedure as for the donation — i.e., start with the same 1,192 AGI goal; key off of 1,000, note the 4,510 EA, and subtract this from the 5,340 in the next cell; the difference in AGI you are resolving for is 5,340−4,510 = 830. Divide 830 by the spread between the AGI columns 1,000 and 1,825, or 825: 830/825 = 1.006. Now multipy 1.006 × 192 = 193, which, added to 4,510, = 4,703. So the new estimated 5-year EA is 4,703.

Index

"A to Z Spending Cuts Plan," 188
accountants, 48, 90, 147–148
actuarial tables, 178
adjusted gross income (AGI):
    average, 14
    charitable donations and, 45–48,
        85–86, 175, 176, 178*n*
    earning assets and, 70, 72–80,
        106–109, 113–114, 125–128,
        149, 167–174, 195–196
    IRS data on, 14, 45–48
    in lifelong financial statements,
        72–80
    net worth and, 57–60, 62, 70,
        123
    spending and, 53, 54, 124
    taxation of, 19, 114, 175
    see also income
affordability:
    definition of, 55
    determination of, 6–7, 48, 67–70,
        93, 104, 106–107, 109, 111,
        115, 124, 127, 168, 174
    income and, 56–60, 67–68, 71
    lifelong financial statements and,
        78–79
    net worth and, 6–7, 79–80, 85
    nonprofits and, 148–149

perceptions of, 6, 17, 101–105,
    108, 130
proof of, 26, 87
spending and, 50, 67–70, 104, 105
American Institute of Certified Public
    Accountants, 148
American People, The (Robey), 57*n*
American Renewal Project, 186
America 2000, 179, 187
AMT (alternative minimum tax),
    162
Aristotle, 36
assets:
    diversification of, *see* diversification
    earning, *see* earning assets
    estimated, 58
    of foundations, 129–132, 140
    gifted, 141
    income and, 99–100
    inflation and, 106, 108–109, 111,
        112–113, 116, 168, 172
    liquidity of, 6, 104, 120, 153, 166
    low-cost, 90, 141, 178
    nonearning, 55, 99–100, 107, 113
    of nonprofits, 129–132, 140,
        149–150
    protection of, 95–100, 119–120
    reduction of, 5, 95–100

assets (*cont.*)
   stability of, 6, 79, 95, 117, 118,
     120, 166
   sufficient, 3, 54
   tax-free transfer of, 153–154
   value of, 4, 7, 55, 73, 80–82, 88,
     90, 92; *see also* net worth
   see also specific assets
Association of Junior Leagues
   International, 32
Astor, Brooke, 42
Atlanta Project (TAP), 182, 192, 198
attorneys, 90, 152, 160
Auten, Gerald, 47

banking, 73, 180
bankruptcy, 52
Baruch, Bernard, 137, 139
Ben & Jerry's Ice Cream, 41, 135
bequests, 152–160
   creating lists for, 152–157
   deferred giving, 143–144
   delicate dipping and, 104
   family foundations vs., 142
   in lifelong financial statements, 71,
     100
   prep sheets for, 153–160
   prioritizing inheritance and,
     155–157
   timing of, 8, 71, 88–89, 100
   updating of, 152
   see also inheritance
Berglas, Steven, 188
Berkshire-Hathaway, 99, 109
Better Business Bureaus, Council of, 91
Bok, Derek, 27
bonds:
   average value of, 56
   in diversified portfolios, 73
   future performance of, 74–77
   historic returns on, 28, 117, 131–
     132
   in inheritances, 155
   interest on, 56, 58
   lowering income from, 113, 114,
     137–139
Bonfire of the Vanities, The (Wolfe),
   37–38

Borowski, Neil, 24–25
breakthroughs, 49–86, 93
   definition of, 14
   financial assumptions of, 122, 124
   on flexible plans, 83–86, 125, 167
   for lifelong financial statements,
     71–82, 84, 86, 100, 113
   on net worth, 55–66, 85
   on spending patterns, 49–54, 85,
     86, 100
   on surplus of wealth, 67–70, 85–86
Brown, Lee, 23
Buddha, 37
Buffett, Warren, 99, 164, 165
bureaucracy, 9, 16, 18, 22
Bush, George, 19
businesses, 19, 20–22, 24
   family feelings in, 41
   income from, 58, 73, 113
   investments by, 30, 31
   learning about, 39
   ownership of, 73
   philanthropy by, 41, 129, 132–136,
     186–188
   profits of, 31, 41, 134, 135
   social environment for, 133–136
   taxation of, 133–134, 135, 175
Business for Social Responsibility,
   186

capital:
   appreciation of, 72, 79, 100,
     103–104, 106, 113, 127, 130,
     139, 144
   depletion of, 95–100, 102–105
   effective use of, 25–26
   spending and, 28, 86, 88
   withdrawal plan for, 103–105, 109,
     110, 112–113, 118, 132
   see also assets
capital gains, 46, 47, 59, 60, 73,
    78, 114, 141, 143, 163–164,
    178n
Carnegie, Andrew, 151, 191, 193
Carter, Jimmy, 182, 189, 192, 193
Carter Center, 192
cash flow, 28, 74–77, 78, 100, 124,
    131, 150

Census Bureau, U.S., 56
Challenges of Wealth (Domini), 98
charities:
    bequests to, 153, 156, 157–160
    concept of, 37–39
    effectiveness of, 22, 37–38
    rankings of, 91
    see also donations, charitable
Christ, Jesus, 37
Christmas Carol, A (Dickens), 193
Christmas in April, 41, 135–136
civic organizations, 23
Clinton, Bill, 12–13, 19
common stock, *see* stocks
communism, 11, 139
community service, 93, 182, 187–188
competition, 19–20, 31, 133, 139,
    180
Concord Coalition, 188
confiscatory taxes, 16, 88
Constitution, U.S., 26
Consumer Price Index, 155
Corporate Giving Directory, 134
corporations:
    philanthropy by, 132–136
    Subchapter-S, 73
    taxation of, 133–134, 175
    see also businesses
cost cutting, 19, 21
Pierre de Coubertin International Fair
    Play Trophy, 183
crime, 12, 13, 27, 187

debt, 101, 104, 120
Declaration of Independence, 26
deficit, budget, 9, 16, 20–21, 35, 139,
    177, 186
deflation, 88, 113
Delancey Street Foundation, 22–24
democracy, 36, 40
depression, 88
Aaron Diamond Foundation, 183
Dickens, Charles, 193
discount rate, 112
diversification:
    aggressive vs. conservative investors
        and, 113
    examples of, 58, 73, 74, 113, 114

protection of wealth by, 88, 113,
    118, 119
risk vs. reward and, 95
"Dollar a Year" executives, 164
Domini, Amy, 98
donations, charitable:
    AGI and, 45–48, 85–86, 175, 176,
        178n
    anonymous, 93
    deferred, 143–144
    incentives for, 178–180
    in-kind, 134
    levels of, 84, 166–174
    lifetime, 89, 100
    net-cost calculation for, 161–163
    net worth and, 14–15, 62–65,
        67–70, 106, 111, 115–116,
        118–119, 122–128, 163–164
    stocks as, 73, 89
    taxation and, 28, 45–48, 89, 96n,
        101, 108, 116, 128, 161–164,
        177–180, 186
    "warehousing" of, 24–25, 30, 179
Dow Jones Industrial Average, 118
dropouts, school, 32
Drucker, Peter F., 12, 30, 178
drug abuse, 12, 13, 23, 30

earning assets (EA):
    AGI and, 70, 72–80, 106–109,
        113–114, 125–128, 149,
        167–174, 195–196
    comparison of, 115–116
    inheritance and, 155, 157
    in lifelong financial statements,
        72–80
    net worth and, 6, 14, 55–60, 62,
        63, 66, 68, 69, 70, 84, 85,
        117–119
    present value of, 114–116, 123
    quality and stability of, 104
earning power, 54, 101, 117, 119,
    166
Economic Recovery Tax Act (ERTA),
    133–134
economy:
    cycles of, 9, 18, 19, 71, 88
    nonprofit, 24–25

economy (*cont.*)
  philanthropy and, 28–30
  potential of, 28–30
education:
  competition and, 133
  philanthropy for, 8, 13, 24, 27,
    32–33, 42, 183–185, 187
  programs for, 32–33
  system of, 11, 24, 30
Education Department, U.S., 11, 13
Einstein, Albert, 110
Ellis, Charles, 72
employee relations, 135–136
equity:
  fixed-income instruments vs.,
    119–120
  investment of, 31, 74–77, 140
  market for, 28, 78
  stability of, 117
ERTA (Economic Recovery Tax Act),
  133–134
estates:
  planning for, 28, 90–91, 151–160
  tax on, 55, 57, 107
  value of, 7, 58
  see also assets
Europe, Eastern, 165

families:
  average income of, 66
  breakdown of, 39
  foundations managed by, 142–143,
    164–165
  low-income, 32–33, 93
  needs of, 6, 8, 12, 27, 167
  philanthropy as influence on, 38–
    44
  values of, 39–40, 192
Federal Bureau of Investigation (FBI),
  12
Federal Reserve Board, 56
finance:
  assumptions in, 122, 124
  constructive habits of, 27–28
  knowledge of, 4, 6, 8, 34, 90
  lifelong statements for, 71–82, 84,
    86, 100, 113

  matrices for, 71–82, 166–174,
    195–196
  one-year statements for, 72–79
  security of, 103, 107, 111–112
  worksheets for, 74–77
financial shelters, 120–121
fixed-income market, 28, 56, 73,
  74–77, 117, 119–120
Forbes, 65, 91
Ford Foundation, 140
Fortune, 151–152
Foundation Center, 129, 131, 186
foundations:
  assets of, 129–132, 140
  educational, 183, 185
  endowments by, 147, 149
  family, 142–143, 164–165
  grants by, 24, 25, 129, 131, 147,
    179, 185
  inflation and, 130, 131, 132, 140
  investments by, 130, 131–132, 179
  net worth of, 130
  philanthropy by, 8, 72, 129–132,
    147, 149
  tax exemptions for, 66, 129
Franklin, Benjamin, 38, 193
free enterprise, 18, 193
Fund for New York City Public
  Education, 183

Galbraith, John Kenneth, 133
Gardner, John W., 43–44, 191–192,
  193
Gates, Bill, 99
Gaul, Gilbert, 24–25
Gibbon, Edward, 12
gifted assets, 141
Give But Give Wisely, 91
Gospel of Wealth, The (Carnegie),
  191
government:
  budget deficit of, 9, 16, 20–21, 35,
    139, 177, 186
  bureaucracy of, 9, 16, 18, 22
  incentives to private sector contrib-
    utors, 178–179
  ineffectiveness of, 12–13

private sector vs., 12–13, 20,
    21–22, 24, 30–31, 181–189
spending levels of, 11, 22, 27, 31,
    139
state and local, 31, 186
Grace Report, 22, 188
Graham, Bob, 40
grants, 24, 25, 129, 131, 147, 179,
    185
Greek society, 36, 193
Greer, Jan, 120

Haas family, 40
Hamilton, Alexander, 193
Head Start, 32–33, 179, 187
health care, 6, 12, 87, 88, 103, 104,
    165, 167
Heilbroner, Robert, 12
Hirschfeld, Ira, 147
homelessness, 11–12
Honeywell Corporation, 184
housing, 104, 153, 167

idiotes, 36
"I Have a Dream" program, 32*n*
imperialism, 36
income:
    adjusted gross (AGI), *see* adjusted
        gross income (AGI)
    affordability and, 56–60, 67–68,
        71
    after-tax, 68–69, 73, 88, 89, 103
    annual, 45–48, 50, 56, 57
    assets and, 99–100
    business, 58, 73, 113
    capitalization of, 56–58, 103
    discretionary, 4, 6, 7, 28, 50, 122,
        124
    earned, 113
    family, 66
    fixed, 28, 56, 73, 74–77, 117,
        119–120
    future, 72–82, 117–120, 124–125
    growth of, 3, 53, 54
    high, 14–15, 45–48, 52, 54, 59,
        60–62, 65, 80, 99, 100
    interest, 28

low-to-medium, 5–6, 11, 32–33,
    45, 47–48, 52, 59, 66, 93,
    99–100, 121–128
net worth and, 6, 14, 48, 55,
    56–60, 62, 67–68, 110, 144
from real estate, 73, 80, 99, 113,
    114
reserves of, 48, 119–120
residual, 50, 62, 66, 130
for savings, 53, 54, 62, 85
spending and, 49–54, 70, 86, 102
stability of, 14, 87–89
sufficient, 3, 124–125
from trusts, 143–144
income taxes, 56, 68–69, 73, 88, 89,
    103, 161, 163, 179, 180
inflation:
    assets and, 106, 108–109, 111,
        112–113, 116, 168, 172
    foundations and, 130, 131, 132,
        140
    interest rates and, 139
    net worth and, 3, 28, 84, 118, 119,
        122–123, 124, 167
    protection against, 3, 9, 28, 71, 78,
        82, 100
    rate of, 65, 78, 79, 114, 117
inheritance:
    affordability and, 79
    built-in adjustments to, 157–160
    earning assets and, 155, 157
    goals for, 6, 17, 124, 151–160
    marriages and, 153
    net worth and, 110
    prep sheets for, 154, 156, 157–160
    priorities in, 34, 39, 102, 155–157
    of real estate, 90
    step-up basis for, 90
    of stocks, 155, 157
    see also bequests; estates
inheritance taxes, 100, 121, 141,
    153–154, 155, 156, 158, 159,
    162
Institute for Policy Innovation, 36*n*
insurance, 90, 166
    health, 88, 103, 104
    life, 100, 153

interest:
  on bonds, 56, 58
  compound, 110
  income from, 28
  mortgage, 58
interest rates, 20
  inflation and, 139
  reduction of, 31
  yields and, 56, 58
Internal Revenue Code (1986), 90
Internal Revenue Service (IRS):
  AGI data from, 14, 45–48
  net worth data from, 7, 8, 55–57,
    62, 109, 113, 178
Investing with the Best (Rosenberg), 146
investments:
  author's experience with, 3, 71, 146
  by businesses, 30, 31
  cash, 74–77
  cycles of, 71, 87–89
  depletion of capital and, 95–98
  diversification of, *see* diversification
    of equity, 31, 74–77, 140
  by foundations, 130, 131–132, 179
  long-term, 140
  markets for, 9, 15, 118, 140
  portfolios of, 73, 110, 113–114,
    131–132, 140, 155
  principal of, 98, 102, 167
  return on, 3, 4, 15, 89, 100,
    111–112, 137–139, 166
  valuation of, 31
  *see also specific securities and
    accounts*
IRAs, 80
"It Profits Us to Strengthen
  Nonprofits" (Drucker), 30

JASS (Judging Affordable Spending
  Sensibly), 67–70, 74–77, 78,
  85–86, 111, 125–128, 148
Jefferson, Thomas, 190–191, 193
job training, 13, 187

Kennedy, Roger, 140
Keroff, H. Peter, 39–40
Keynes, John Maynard, 20
kindergartens, 183

Koldyke, Martin, 184
Krasnanski, Marvin L., 133–134

labor unions, 23, 187
Lang, Gene, 32n
"Leadership and Development" retreat, 184
Levi Strauss, 41, 135
Levy, John, 152
life, quality of, 19, 23–24, 65, 86
life expectancy, 89, 104
liquidity, 6, 104, 120, 153, 166
literacy, 12
Littlefield, Ed, 40–41
lobbyists, 36n, 189
lotteries, 112
luxuries, 50, 52
Lynch, Peter, 38

MacArthur Foundation, 182
Machiavelli, Niccolò, 36
mailings, 35–36
Maimonides, 37
Manhattan Institute for Policy
  Research, 186
marriages, 38, 40, 73, 153
"Marshall Plan for America," 13
Melville Innovations Grants Program,
  24
Microsoft, 99, 109
money:
  constructive use of, 3, 28, 100
  decision-making on, 28
  "game" of, 92–93
  present value of, 112–116
  as "root of all evil," 34
  surplus, 8, 13, 16
  time value of, 110–116
Money, 91
Moore, Jeffrey, 60–61
Mormons, 173
mortgages, 58, 120
Muhammad, 37
multimillionaires, 84, 92
mutual funds, 118, 144

National Center for Neighborhood
  Enterprise, 21

National Charities Information
  Bureau, 91
National Civic League's "American
  Renewal Project," 186
National Philanthropic Advisory
  Service (PAS), 91
National Urban League, 13
net worth, 55–66
  affordability and, 6–7, 79–80, 85
  age and, 103–105, 160
  AGI and, 57–60, 62, 70, 123
  breakthrough on, 55–66, 85
  calculation of, 14, 55–60, 85, 107,
    109
  charitable donations and, 14–15,
    62–65, 67–70, 106, 111,
    115–116, 118–119, 122–128,
    163–164
  definition of, 6, 55
  depletion of capital and, 96–98,
    103–105
  earning assets and, 6, 14, 55–60,
    62, 63, 66, 68, 69, 70, 84, 85,
    117–119
  financial security and, 103, 107,
    111–112
  of foundations, 130
  income and, 6, 14, 48, 55, 56–60,
    62, 67–68, 110, 144
  inflation and, 3, 28, 84, 118, 119,
    122–123, 124, 167
  IRS data on, 7, 8, 55–57, 62, 109,
    113, 178
  low-to-medium, 6, 121–128
  negative, 101
  projections of, 71–82, 85, 88,
    117–120, 125–128
  proportionate, 59
  relative, 123
  risks to, 117–119
  sample calculation of, 57–59
New Economics, 18
New Jersey Supreme Court, 133
Newman, Paul, 135
New Vision High School, 183
New York Times, 42
nonearning assets, 55, 99–100, 107,
  113

nonprofit organizations:
  accounting methods of, 147–148
  annual reports of, 149
  assets of, 129–132, 140, 149–150
  budget deficits and, 177
  diversity of, 38
  effectiveness of, 22–25, 30–31,
    146–150, 175, 176, 190–191
  for-profit organizations vs., 30, 187
  investigation of, 146–150
  management of, 21, 22, 146,
    147–150
  nonprofit status of, 179
  solicitations by, 35–36, 41, 92
  tax exemptions for, 24–25, 149, 175
  "warehousing" by, 24–25, 30, 179
  see also charities; donations, chari-
    table; foundations
North American Free Trade
  Agreement, 139

Olympic Games, 183
O'Neil, John, 89

R. B. Pamplin Corporation, 41
Paradox of Success, The (O'Neil), 89
pensions, 59, 80
Pensions and Investments Age, 134
Philadelphia Inquirer, 24–25
Philanthropic Initiative, Inc., 39–40
philanthropy:
  arguments for and against, 87–94
  author's experience with, 3–5, 7, 8,
    42–43
  by businesses, 41, 129, 132–136,
    186–188
  computer models for, 8, 71, 128
  conservatism in, 45–48, 68, 72, 85,
    90–91, 109, 128, 130, 132, 166,
    173
  cost-effectiveness of, 161–165
  definition of, 37–39
  depletion of wealth and, 72,
    95–100
  discernment in, 35–36, 145–150
  economic impact of, 28–30
  for education, 8, 13, 24, 27, 32–33,
    42, 183–185, 187

philanthropy (*cont.*)
  effectiveness of, 25–33
  families influenced by, 38–44
  financial commitment to, 83–85
  flexible plan for, 83–86, 125, 167
  by foundations, 8, 22, 129–132,
    147, 149
  goals for, 82, 91, 167–168
  guidelines for, 186–189
  as habit, 8–9, 16, 27–28, 92, 143

philanthropy (*cont.*)
  insecurities about, 87–91
  insufficient level of, 14–16, 40–41,
    45–48, 62–66
  leadership in, 21–25, 186–188,
    191–192
  living expenses and, 4, 50–52, 53,
    78, 79, 82, 85, 87–88, 100, 104,
    108, 113, 121, 152, 169
  for local communities, 25, 39, 93,
    182, 187–188
  mathematical analysis of, 15*n*, 82
  motivations for, 37–38
  national advisory board on, 185–
    186
  negative connotations of, 27,
    35–36, 37
  opportunity costs and, 164–165
  options for, 141–144
  personal satisfaction from, 8, 31,
    34–44, 71
  potential for, 14, 25–26, 31–32,
    166–174
  priorities in, 145–146
  procrastination and, 89
  professional advice on, 90, 92
  role models for, 38–44, 190–194
  social impact of, 9, 11–26, 27,
    30–33, 36, 37–38, 65, 108,
    133–136, 164–165, 175–194
  timing of, 28, 137–140
Pickle Family Circus, 43
Plato, 36
portfolios, 73, 110, 113–114,
    131–132, 140, 155
poverty, 11, 12
pregnancies, teenage, 32

Preliminary Tax Return Data (1991),
    45–48
preschools, 183–184
present value, 112–116
principal, invading of, 98, 102, 167
prisons, 23, 30
private sector:
  effectiveness of, 16, 31–32
  fundraising in, 13
  public sector vs., 12–13, 20, 21–22,
    24, 30–31, 181–189
Progressive Policy Institute, 188
Projection of Finances Worksheet, 72,
    74–77
property taxes, 100, 151
property values, 120
public sector, *see* government
purchasing power, 88, 100, 118, 124

"rainy-day funds," 119–120
Reaching Out Coalition, 186–189
Reaching Out philosophy, 18–33, 34,
    41–42, 44, 94, 135, 145, 146,
    176, 186, 191, 193, 194
Reaganomics, 18
real estate:
  income from, 73, 80, 99, 113, 114
  inheritance of, 90
  market for, 28, 31, 65, 73, 118, 120
  sales of, 100
  taxation of, 100, 151
recession, 18
refinancing, 120
rehabilitation programs, 23–24
religion, 37, 39, 42, 45, 65, 173
retail, 137
Robey, Bryant, 57*n*
role models, 38–44, 190–194
Roman society, 36
Rosenberg, Louise, 42–43, 82
Rosenwald, Julius, 165
royalties, 58
Rudney, Gabriel, 47
Russian emigrés, 42–43

salaries, 59, 73, 74–77, 113, 114
S&P Stock Index. *See* Standard &
    Poor 500 Stock Index

savings, 28
  amount of, 49–54, 55
  bank accounts for, 73
  income for, 53, 54, 62, 85
scholarships, 184
school districts, 184–185
self-deprivation, 5–6, 101–105
self-esteem, 37–38, 40
shareholders, 31, 132–133, 135
shelters, financial, 120–121
"Should You Leave It All to Your
    Children?," 151–152
Silbert, Mimi, 23–24
Smith Manufacturing v. Barlow, 133
Social Security, 59
Social Venture Network, 186
SOI ("Statistics of Income"), 56
solicitations, 35–36, 41, 92
Soros, George, 164, 165
special-interest groups, 21–22, 36,
    188
spending:
  affordability and, 50, 67–70, 104,
    105
  AGI and, 53, 54, 124
  capital and, 28, 86, 88
  discretionary, 4, 7, 31, 79, 122
  government, 11, 22, 27, 31, 139
  income and, 49–54, 70, 86, 102
  increase in, 6, 16, 85, 86, 173
  patterns of, 49–54, 85, 86, 100
  relative, 50–52
Standard & Poor 500 Stock Index, 15,
    56, 58, 65, 118, 139
Stanford University, 43
start-ups, 185–186
"Statistics of Income" (SOI), 56
stocks:
  appreciation of vs. return on, 79,
    99, 103, 143
  asset-value calculations for, 58
  average market value of, 56
  as charitable donations, 73, 89
  dividends from, 28, 58, 109, 114,
    132–133, 143
  in diversified portfolios, 73
  historic returns on, 117, 139
  in inheritances, 155, 157

lowering income from, 79, 99, 103,
    114, 143
  options and, 120
  price-earnings multiples on, 31
"Success By Six" (SBS) plan, 184
Supply-Side economics, 18

Taft Group, 134
TAP (The Atlanta Project), 182, 198,
    192
Task Force on Private Sector
    Initiatives, 133
taxation, taxes:
  of AGI, 19, 114, 175
  alternative minimum (AMT), 162
  brackets for, 7, 8, 14–15, 19, 85,
    123, 172–173, 174, 175
  of businesses, 133–134, 135, 175
  charitable donations and, 28,
    45–48, 89, 96*n*, 101, 108, 116,
    128, 161–164, 177–180, 186
  confiscatory, 16, 88
  constructive use of money and, 28,
    100
  decreases in, 18, 19
  deductions in, 16, 19, 28, 30, 48,
    67, 68, 78, 89, 107, 126, 142,
    150, 162, 164, 173, 177, 178,
    180
  estate, 55, 57, 107
  exemptions in, 24–25, 56, 66,
    129, 133–134, 149, 164,
    175
  income, 56, 68–69, 73, 88, 89,
    103, 161, 163, 179, 180
  increases in, 16, 18–19, 20, 163,
    193
  inheritance, 100, 121, 141,
    153–154, 155, 156, 158, 159,
    162
  legislation on, 26, 161, 177–180
  loopholes in, 180
  penalties in, 178
  professional advice on, 48, 106
  property, 100, 151
  rate of, 79, 108, 113, 162, 163,
    169, 172
  revenues from, 30, 31, 34, 178, 179

taxation, taxes (*cont.*)
  shelters for, 50, 72, 120–121
  state and local, 114, 161, 173
  transfer of assets and, 153–154
  voluntary, 194
teachers, 184
Teen Outreach Program (TOP), 32
telephone solicitations, 35
time value of money, 110–116
tithes, 65, 127, 173
Tocqueville, Alexis de, 181
Treasury Department, U.S., 30, 56
Treasury securities, 119, 139
Trickle Down policies, 18–19,192–193
trusts, 58, 88, 90, 141, 143–144, 152,
    160
tuition, 187

unemployment, 12, 13, 19, 31, 187
United States:
  affluence of, 65
  associations in, 181
  budget deficit of, 9, 16, 20–21, 35,
      139, 177, 186
  decline of, 11–14
  economic philosophy of, 11, 18–19
  immigrants to, 42–43
  infrastructure of, 18, 135, 139
  national debt of, 11
  political system of, 11, 26, 36, 40
  predominance of, 11, 17, 20, 26
  values of, 39–40, 181–183, 190–194
"units," 92

Variability of Charitable Giving by the
    Wealthy, The (Auten and
    Rudney), 47
voluntary taxes, 194

volunteerism, 20, 32, 38, 41, 93, 134,
    135–136, 181, 182, 187–188,
    190–191
voting, 190

wages, 59, 73, 114, 139
Wall Street Journal, 30
Wal-Mart, 109
"Warehouses of Wealth: The Tax-Free
    Economy" (Gaul and Borowski),
    24–25
wealth:
  accumulation of, 3, 14, 48, 55,
      57
  average, 71–72
  concentration of, 191
  definition of, 54
  depletion of, 5, 71, 72, 95–100
  human worth and, 92–93
  insecurity about, 6, 87–91
  levels of, 54, 115–116, 128
  problems of, 6, 39–40, 71, 87–91,
      118–119
  relative, 59–60, 65, 80–82, 92, 128
  surplus, 27, 28–30, 34, 48, 50,
      67–70, 85–86, 98, 106, 108
  see also net worth
wealthy:
  generosity of, 4–5, 7, 14–16, 26,
      28, 34–44, 62–66
  lifestyle of, 3, 5–6, 17, 101–105
  self-deprivation and, 5–6, 101–
      105
Wei, Tim, 60
wills, 152, 157–160
  see also bequests
Wolfe, Tom, 37–38
Woodson, Robert L., 21
Worth, 38